THE WIDOW'S HUSBAND

Borgo Press Books by FRANK J. MORLOCK

Chuzzlewit
Congreve's Comedy of Manners
Crime and Punishment
Falstaff (with William Shakespeare, John Dennis, and William Kendrick)
Fathers and Sons
The Idiot
Jurgen
Justine
Lord Jim
Notes from the Underground
Oblomov
Outrageous Women: Lady Macbeth and Other French Plays (editor and translator)
Peter and Alexis
The Princess Casamassima
A Raw Youth
The Stendhal Hamlet Scenarios and Other Shakespearean Shorts from the French (editor and translator)
The Widow's Husband; and, Porthos in Search of an Outfit: Two Dumasian Comedies (editor and translator)

THE WIDOW'S HUSBAND

AND, PORTHOS IN SEARCH OF AN OUTFIT: TWO DUMASIAN COMEDIES

FRANK J. MORLOCK,

EDITOR

THE BORGO PRESS
MMXII

Copyright © 2001, 2012 by Frank J. Morlock

FIRST EDITION

Published by Wildside Press LLC

www.wildsidebooks.com

For Harry Hayfield

CONTENTS

THE WIDOW'S HUSBAND: A COMEDY IN ONE ACT,
   by Alexandre Dumas 9
CAST OF CHARACTERS. 11
THE WIDOW'S HUSBAND 13
PORTHOS IN SEARCH OF AN OUTFIT: A COMEDY
   IN ONE ACT, by Auguste Anicet-Bourgeois, Philippe
   Dumanoir, and Édouard Brisebarre. 121
CAST OF CHARACTERS. 123
PORTHOS IN SEARCH OF AN OUTFIT. 125
ABOUT THE AUTHOR 213

THE WIDOW'S HUSBAND: A COMEDY IN ONE ACT
BY ALEXANDRE DUMAS

For Michael Lidsky

CAST OF CHARACTERS

de Vertpre

Leon Auvray, Pauline's intended

Adele (Mrs. de Vertpre)

Pauline, Adele's niece

Helene, Adele's Chambermaid

THE WIDOW'S HUSBAND

A small boudoir. To the left a door communicating with Mme de Vertpre's apartment. To the right, the door of Pauline's apartment, also further back on the right, a chimney. In the rear, a double doors communicating with the outside. In the corner to the right, a second door. In the opposite corner, a window giving on a park. In the forestage, a table and on it an open album with a crayon.

At rise, a bell rings twice, in Mme de Vertpre's room followed impatiently by calls of "Helene! Helene!"

Mme de Vertpre enters from her room as Helene enters from the other. Mme de Vertpre is in mourning clothes—she tosses a scarf she has in her hand on an armchair.

ADELE

Well, Miss! I rang, I called and you didn't come. What were you doing if you please?

HELENE

I was dressing, Miss Pauline.

ADELE

Go down and get my mail. I am expecting one impatiently and I just saw the mail man enter.

HELENE

(opening the door to go down) Here's Joseph; bring the letters up.

ADELE

Take them and give them to me. That's fine.

HELENE

Can I go back to Miss Pauline?

ADELE

No—stay here.

(reading the address) "Mme de Vertpre—

(tosses the letter away)—"Madame Adele de Vertpre"—that's his writing.

(opening it) Today—he'll arrive today. Dear Paul! Come, Helene, and listen carefully to what I am going to tell you—; this morning, a gentleman of thirty-five or thirty-six will present himself to speak with me; if I am with someone, you will inform me; if I am alone—you will show him in.

HELENE

Does Madame wish to tell me his name?

ADELE

It's unnecessary; you will recognize him without being named. Except for Mr. Leon Auvray, Pauline's fiancé, who comes to visit us every day in this country—I don't receive anyone—so—

HELENE

If I am mistaken, then Madame won't be angry with me—?

ADELE

Brown hair, black eyes, middle-size figure—that's his appearance, keep it in mind.

HELENE

If Mr. Leon is with Madame—that doesn't matter?

ADELE

No—doubtless.

HELENE

But if Madame is at her toilette?

ADELE

You will lead him to me!

HELENE

Without informing you?

ADELE

Without informing me.

HELENE

I ask Madame's pardon for all my questions, but Madame is not accustomed to receive everyone.

ADELE

The person I'm expecting is not everyone.

HELENE

I mean to say strangers.

ADELE

This gentleman is not a stranger.

HELENE

(going)

Madame can be easy; as soon as her relative arrives—

ADELE

I'm not expecting relatives.

HELENE

(knowingly)

Then I understand.

ADELE

You misunderstand.

HELENE

He's—

ADELE

My husband, Miss.

HELENE

Madame's husband? Why, everyone thinks she's a widow.

ADELE

Why, all the world is mistaken. Now, listen, as your indiscreet questions, your more indiscreet suppositions, are forcing me into a confidence in you that I don't plan to make, you will have the goodness to keep silent—for—at the slightest indiscretion, you hear—at the slightest, I will be obliged to send you away, Helene; and that, despite the affection I bear you—for this secret is not mine alone and it could compromise a person who is dearer to me than myself.

HELENE

Oh! Madame, be certain—

ADELE

That's fine. Now you've been warned, so be discreet.

(half going into her room)

See how it is.

HELENE

Mr. Leon. Ought I to tell him you are not here?

ADELE

No, tell him to wait for me. Then you will come give me my hat.

(goes into her room)

LEON

(rapping on the door which is in the corner on the right)

Can I come in?

HELENE

Yes.

LEON

(half opening the door)

Alone?

HELENE

Alone.

LEON

It seems to me I heard the voice of Mme de Vertpre.

HELENE

She was here just now, and while waiting for you—

LEON

She went back into her room, which means she won't receive me this morning.

HELENE

Well, to the contrary, she begs you to wait until she's finished dressing.

LEON

She told you that?

HELENE

Yes, sir—

(she gets ready to go into Adele's room)

LEON

(stops her—by the end of a scarf she's taken from the armchair which Adele had left there—and sits down)

Listen, Helene.

HELENE

What?

LEON

Mme de Vertpre's spoken to you about me? Listen!

HELENE

Right now.

LEON

(playing with the scarf and kissing it)

And she told you?

HELENE

What are you doing?

LEON

Whose scarf is this?

HELENE

My mistress's.

LEON

And it touched her neck, her shoulders! I envy it and I kiss it.

HELENE

But sir—it's not the scarf you are kissing, those are my hands.

LEON

(rising) That's because your hands are so pretty, Helene.

HELENE

You're crazy.

LEON

I am amorous—

HELENE

Of my hands?

LEON

A bit. Of your mistress—a lot.

HELENE

(aside)

Poor young man!

(aloud) And Miss Pauline, your fiancé?

LEON

She's a charming person.

HELENE

Whom you love also?

LEON

Like a sister.

HELENE

That won't count with her; for I think she loves you otherwise than a brother.

LEON

Heavens, now that's what worries me, and sometimes makes me so sad.

HELENE

(laughing)

You! Ah! For goodness sakes!

LEON

But also, why the Devil doesn't Mme de Vertpre consider that to marry her niece is a bad way to keep her by her? Certainly before having seen your mistress, I loved Pauline with all my soul—but since that period, since I've seen the two of them side by side; despite myself, I am making comparisons. They are both pretty, but Mme de Vertpre has something spicy in her beauty. Both are sparkling wits—but Mme de Vertpre's wit is completed by a worldly sophistication which Pauline's lacks. Each of them has an excellent character, but little Pauline gets irritated and pouts; Mme de Vertpre on the contrary, is always gracious. Pauline loves me, I know it—but without being fatuous, Mme de Vertpre doesn't detest me, she grants me out loud the title of friend—in going back over our walks, our discussions—the little services that she demands of me constantly, and that I am so happy to perform for her—and more—well, that makes you laugh?

HELENE

Would you pretend to marry Mme de Vertpre?

LEON

Why not?

HELENE

Pardon, it's that—

(laughing)

LEON

Isn't she a widow?

HELENE

Ah! That's true; I was forgetting that.

(a bell rings in Mme de Vertpre's room)

Look, they're calling me—I'm gossiping with you and I'm going to get a scolding.

LEON

You will tell your mistress that I kept you to tell you how charming she is—and she will pardon you.

HELENE

Don't worry....

(going into Mme de Vertpre's room)

LEON

It's not bad to tell secrets to the maid—the mistress always gets to learn something. Then she was worried I was coming and she said I should stay! It's just that a lady's toilette takes so long. If at least there were a newspaper here, ah, Mme de Vertpre's album. A blank page, a pencil—(opens the album)—it's a challenge!

(Takes the pencil and writes—Pauline enters on tiptoe, gets behind Leon's chair, and reads over his shoulder.)

PAULINE

(reading) Oh—never shorten these hours that I wish for.

LEON

(abruptly closing the album)

Ah! It's you.

PAULINE

Did I scare you?

LEON

You can't think that.

PAULINE

What are you writing?

LEON

Nothing.

PAULINE

Verse.

LEON

A keepsake.

PAULINE

For whom?

LEON

You ask that!

PAULINE

Let's see them.

LEON

Why, no.

PAULINE

Why, yes, I beg you, Mr. Leon; I'm getting annoyed.

LEON

I wanted to finish them before showing them to you—for you especially, Pauline.

PAULINE

It will be your first thought and it's always the best.
Oh—never shorten the hours that I desire.
Grant them to me;
God gives you the power.
To hear you and to see you is my life—
Allow me to hear you and see you.

(repeating) To hear you and see you.

LEON

Poetry has a language of its own—it touches God, and God doesn't mind.

PAULINE

That's true.

(offers him her hand)

And I won't be more susceptible than he.
As the air in passing—
Removes the shadows from heaven—
Without a trace
Your eyes fixed on mine—

Leave on my face—
Your long black hair—

What's this mean, sir?—

LEON

Ah—yes—face and trace—the rhyme isn't very fine, is it? I was telling you the verse needed to be corrected.

PAULINE

But that's not it.

LEON

What is it, then?

PAULINE

Leave in my face your long black hair. My black hair?

LEON

(aside) Ah! Blessings—she's a blonde, and a superb blonde at that.

(aloud) My God—why, it's that!

PAULINE

Why, it's that these verses were for someone else, that's all.

LEON

I swear to you.

PAULINE

Indeed, why would these verses be for me? And why would you be writing verses to me?

LEON

Why, it's an inconceivable distraction I intended to write blonde—the pencil twisted in my fingers.

PAULINE

(with bitterness) Ah, yes, long and blonde—you are right, sir, these verses need to be corrected—their harmony is strange.

(she returns the album to Leon)

LEON

(aside) Decidedly, I'm embroiling myself.

(aloud) Pauline.

PAULINE

Oh—be careful to speak to me in prose, sir.

LEON

Miss—come on, now she's crying.

PAULINE

Not at all—I am not crying, you are mistaken.

LEON

To the devil with poetry! For goodness sakes—it's the first and last time. Listen to me. This verse—

PAULINE

Why, who's talking to you about those verses, for heaven's sake? Why, I'm not thinking of them anymore at all! I—I—Oh! My God, how unhappy I am—

(entwining herself in an armchair)

LEON

I beg you—I beg you—

PAULINE

Leave me alone—you make me lose patience and I detest you. Am I not free to weep if I am sad? Why, this is tyranny!

(throwing herself in to Mme de Vertpre's arms as she enters)

ADELE

(entering)

What's wrong with you?

PAULINE

Oh—I am really unhappy—

LEON

(bowing) Madame!

ADELE

I thank you, Mr. Leon, for having waited for me—what is it, Pauline? Another quarrel, a sulking fit?

PAULINE

Oh, this time, it's not my fault, auntie—if you knew—

ADELE

(to Leon) Did you think of me?

LEON

Of you? Always.

ADELE

When I say of me, it's my commission, I mean.

LEON

Your portrait? Here it is, Madame, delightful, beautiful, shining with freshness—and yet so strong beneath.

ADELE

Flatterer! Give it to me.

LEON

(giving her the portrait) Already!

ADELE

Look here, Pauline, do you think it resembles me?

PAULINE

(without looking) Yes, auntie.

ADELE

Say, do you think you've seen it? You are sulking, Pauline! Come with us, it will distract you.

PAULINE

Thanks.

LEON

You are going out, Madame.

ADELE

Yes, now that's why I begged you to wait for me; I need your arm.

PAULINE

That's it; he won't even stay so I can scold him. Oh, I am really sacrificed!

LEON

And where are we going?

ADELE

On the main road, I am expecting someone I haven't seen in a long while, so I really want to see them again and I'm going to before—

LEON

Him or her?

ADELE

(meaningful) Him!

LEON

(jealously) Ah! Have you noticed the weather?

ADELE

(going to the window) A bit cloudy.

LEON

Black like ink.

ADELE

You're afraid of the rain and you refuse to be my chevalier?

LEON

Me, Madame?

ADELE

I demand a service from you, and when it's a question of doing it for me, a few drops of water frighten you?

LEON

A few drops of water frighten me? Why, for you I would cross the straits of Lestros—let's go, Madame, let's go.

ADELE

Decidedly, Pauline, you are not coming.

PAULINE

Decidedly, Auntie, I'm staying.

ADELE

Well, listen—she's going to tell me the cause of your quarrel—I will scold her and I will bring her back, submissive and repentant—goodbye, dear child.

(he hugs her)

PAULINE

Bye, Auntie.

LEON

Au revoir, Miss.

PAULINE

Au revoir, sir.

(Leon and Adele leave.)

(alone) Yes, scold him, auntie; but it seems to me it was up to me to scold him and not you. With you, he's always pleasant, urgent, gallant, but with me, as I must be his wife, he's quite at ease not to dissemble.

(going to the table on which the album is placed and taking it) Verses, they're pretty, his verses! A lawyer who makes poetry! And as for me, madwoman, who had thought they were for me, and found them charming—! Ah, my God—now the page is torn. Bah! It's no great difficulty, he will rewrite them on another. Ah, yes, but on the back of a watercolor by Descamps! My God—what's auntie going to say—? And why does he write verse on the back of a watercolor anyway? As if he'd done it several times and no one noticed it—yes, but if she noticed it in my room—so much the worse—verse and watercolor in the fire.

(the page burns) Oh—I think the design was only pasted on the page. You could replace it on another.

(she tries to pull it out of the fire) Come on—now, I"m going to burn myself—why, I don't know what I'm doing, I'm crazy, I've lost my head.

HELENE

(entering) Oh! My God—how chagrining!

PAULINE

Yes, I'm chagrined, yes, I'm unhappy, but I will have courage, and I won't love him anymore!

HELENE

And why don't you love him anymore?

PAULINE

Because he loves someone else. Do you conceive, Helene? To love a brunette—a woman who has black hair—what wretched taste!

HELENE

(looking in a mirror) Why, no—it seems not so ugly to me!

PAULINE

(coming to herself) Oh, why you, Helene, you have black hair, a very beautiful black.

HELENE

And Madame, your aunt has black hair, too.

PAULINE

Heavens, it's true—that auntie—

HELENE

She's pretty, your aunt—

PAULINE

Oh—my God, you're right, Helene—my aunt's a brunette—she's pretty, she's a widow—hardly a few years older than me—those verses were in my aunt's album—the thousand kindnesses that he has for her—their conversations, their walks—in this moment—why, in this moment again they are together—oh, Helene—he loves my aunt; it's my aunt he will marry.

HELENE

Listen, it's possible that Mr. Leon loves Mme de Vertpre, but I'll answer for it. He won't marry her.

PAULINE

You're sure of it?

HELENE

Very sure.

PAULINE

And how's that? Tell me, I beg you my little Helene.

HELENE

Because Mme de Vertpre isn't—

(aside) Ah, my God, what was I going to say?

PAULINE

Isn't what?

HELENE

That's what I'm forbidden to tell you—but, still—there's a God for lovers—and that's who will avenge you.

PAULINE

How's that—?

HELENE

You see the rain?

PAULINE

Well—

HELENE

Didn't you tell me they were going for a walk?

PAULINE

(going to the window) Oh, yes, it's true, they are going to be wet, soaked to the bone, and I will be satisfied, enchanted. Look, look there, Helene—do you see them returning? How they are running—Leon's hat blew off. How amusing they are! What excellent rain!

HELENE

Which soaks her aunt and her fiancé. Excellent little heart.

PAULINE

(laughing) That's not it at all—it's that there hadn't been any rain for a long while—the earth was very parched and this sudden shower was very necessary for the harvest.

(she runs off laughing)

HELENE

A little nut who laughs and cries at the same time—how Mr. Leon's in for it.

(Soaked, Leon and Adele enter hurriedly.)

ADELE

Helene! Helene! Quick, help me!

LEON

(asking) Indeed, I told you, it's not my fault—

ADELE

Oh—big deal! I will change my dress, that's all. Come Helene—oh—I'm cold—quick! Quick!

(goes with Helene into her room)

LEON

(alone) You will change your dress—that's very fine—but as for me, I won't change my clothes. And that for an excellent reason. To the devil with promenading! It's that I am soaked. She has a cold! Me too, by God! I am shivering.

(stopping in front of the fire) All the same, I am really good to fuss. Here's the fire, and I am all alone—while she's changing I don't see very much why I deprive myself of drying my clothes. Yes, that's an excellent idea.

(he takes off his coat, placing it by the fire on the back of a chair and sits astride the chair) There—let's not lose sight of the chamber door and at the least voice—my word, if the gentleman to whom we were going is out in weather like that, I give him my sincere compliment. And if he's coming through the park, it would be very nice of him to bring me back my hat.

(turning, hearing someone) What is this?

(A servant followed by de Vertpre, with an overnight bag. The servant places the bag on a chair and leaves—Leon, back turned to the door, doesn't notice this.)

De VERTPRE

Pardon, sir—I am probably deceived.

LEON

(without disturbing himself) That's possible, sir.

De VERTPRE

I thought I was entering the home of Mme de Vertpre.

LEON

You are here.

De VERTPRE

But doubtless she is not?

LEON

(pointing to Mme de Vertpre's room) Indeed, she is there.

De VERTPRE

(going towards the door) Thanks.

LEON

(stopping him) Pardon! It's that she is changing her dress.

De VERTPRE

Ah! And you—you're changing clothes, as it appears?

LEON

No, I don't have the good luck to have one to change into and I am content to dry it. I must tell you that the two of us were soaked to the bone—you'll excuse me, won't you?

(goes back to the chimney)

De VERTPRE

Certainly!

(aside) Who the devil is this gentleman who is so at ease in my house?

LEON

As for you, you are not soaked?

De VERTPRE

I came from Paris in a carriage. I was in a great hurry to see Mme de Vertpre.

LEON

Ah! Yes—is it you she's expecting? Yes, yes—she's expecting a gentleman. I am going to inform her.

(going toward Mme de Vertpre's door)

De VERTPRE

What! You are going to enter Mme de Vertpre's room while she's changing her dress?

LEON

No, I am going to tell her through the door.

De VERTPRE

Thanks, I'll wait.

LEON

Then take the trouble to sit down.

De VERTPRE

You are too good. So, Mme de Vertpre told you she was

expecting me?

LEON

Yes—this morning—she spoke of it in the air—

De VERTPRE

She added that it was pressing business?

LEON

No—she didn't add that.

(he rings—a servant enters) Joseph—some wood—

De VERTPRE

(aside) Very good!

(aloud) Sir, the matter I must discuss with Mme de Vertpre is secret.

LEON

That may be, sir—

De VERTPRE

So that unless you are her husband—

LEON

I don't have that honor, sir—

De VERTPRE

I will dare expect from your discretion—

LEON

That I retire, right?

De VERTPRE

If you would be so complacent.

LEON

Tell me—will you be a long while?

De VERTPRE

Why's that?

LEON

Ah—because you will upset our whole day.

De VERTPRE

I will be brief.

LEON

Thanks—you are being very likable.

(going to leave)

De VERTPRE

And your coat?

LEON

(returning and taking his coat) I am going to finish drying it in Helene's room.

(Leon exits)

De VERTPRE

(watching Leon move away) Now, there's a very original young man, and if I were the jealous type—now he's gone, I think I can go into my wife's room.

(raps on the door)

ADELE

(voice from her room) Don't be impatient, Leon, I am ready.

De VERTPRE

Leon! Eh, by Jove! Madame, it's not Leon, it's me.

ADELE

Ah—it's his voice.

(she rushes on stage) Dear friend—dear Paul—with what impatience I was awaiting you—

De VERTPRE

Lonely, Adele?

ADELE

Oh! Yes—

De VERTPRE

Come on—kiss me then. You are always beautiful, dear friend! And you thought of me?

ADELE

Since I received your letter that informed me of your arrival at Havre, I counted the hours, the minutes, and but for this strange secret you confided to me, I would have told the whole world of my happiness.

De VERTPRE

This secret is still necessary. But tell me—what is this—?

ADELE

But the political circumstances have really changed!

De VERTPRE

Changed, changed—when I got here, there was a young man—

ADELE

Your crossing was pleasant?

De VERTPRE

Eighteen days from New York to Havre—this young man—who was—?

ADELE

All the same, it tired you. You need rest. I am going to give instructions.

De VERTPRE

No, I assure you, I don't feel tired in the least. As I arrived, I found a young man here—

ADELE

Ah! Yes, Leon.

De VERTPRE

Who is this Leon?

ADELE

A charming young man.

De VERTPRE

I saw him, and as to that—my opinion.

ADELE

Very witty—

De VERTPRE

I spoke to him—and still.

ADELE

Distinguished lawyer—

De VERTPRE

Are you involved in a lawsuit?

ADELE

No, sir—but I have a niece—

De VERTPRE

And so—?

ADELE

—A niece to marry.

De VERTPRE

And this young man—?

ADELE

Comes here for Pauline.

De VERTPRE

You know what I say?

ADELE

Me, my friend? Ah!

De VERTPRE

It's very delicate what I have to tell you—

ADELE

Never mind.

De VERTPRE

I've just noticed this young man, only said a few words to him.

ADELE

Well—?

De VERTPRE

Well, I would swear he isn't coming here for Pauline—

ADELE

For goodness sakes! Who, then?

De VERTPRE

For a charming woman, beautiful as an angel, fresh as a young girl—and witty—all the lawyers in the world—for Madame, the widow Adele de Vertpre, my wife.

ADELE

Oh, why, you're crazy, my poor Paul! You do eighteen leagues to see me, and after you arrive, instead of telling me about yourself, of your trips, of your plans—you continue to want the rumor of your death spread about—

De VERTPRE

Later, dear friend, I will talk to you about all that—but for the moment, you see, I have an idea. Mr. Leon—

ADELE

Comes here for Pauline.

De VERTPRE

I ask nothing better than to believe it, but—

ADELE

You want proof of it—?

De VERTPRE

Proof wouldn't be unpleasant to me—and right now, if that is possible.

ADELE

Well, sir—since that is what concerns you, seeing me again, I am going to give you this proof. Let's see, what can I do? Ah! Here, hide in there.

(pointing to the door to her room)

De VERTPRE

And then?

ADELE

I will make him come; I will tell him to explain his intentions, and you will hear him repeat to me the confession of his love for Pauline and ask me for her hand.

De VERTPRE

That will be very fine.

ADELE

I haven't seen him—I won't see him. I am going to have him called—and then we will set the day for the marriage contract.

De VERTPRE

I will sign it with pleasure.

ADELE

(ringing) Helene!

(Helene enters.)

ADELE

Inform Mr. Leon that I want to speak to him, and announce him when he comes.

(Helene leaves.)

De VERTPRE

Marvelous, dear friend.

ADELE

And after this proof, you will doubtless allow me to give you what for at my leisure.

De VERTPRE

You are the best of women.

ADELE

You're a jealous fool.

De VERTPRE

Me!

ADELE

And you deserve that I not give you—

De VERTPRE

What?

ADELE

(pointing to the portrait Leon gave her)

Look!

De VERTPRE

(taking the portrait) Your picture, ah!

ADELE

Which I made to give you and that I made exactly to fit the same frame as yours, so that even absent, we would be united.

De VERTPRE

You are completely charming, and I will be enchanted to be wrong in my suspicions and to ask your pardon and kiss your feet.

ADELE

On your knees, then.

De VERTPRE

After the interview.

ADELE

Incredulous!

HELENE

(announcing) Mr. Leon.

ADELE

Quick into this room, and be all ears.

De VERTPRE

I won't lose a word of the interview. I'll answer for that.

ADELE

That's fine. You are going to see who he loves.

(De Vertpre enters the room to the left.)

ADELE

Helene, show him in and leave us.

LEON

How grateful I am to you, Madame, for having called me after you got rid of your irritation!

ADELE

What do you mean, sir?

LEON

He really bored you, didn't he? I suspected so! He didn't have an amusing manner at all—

ADELE

Why, sir—you don't know the man.

LEON

And I feel no wish to make his acquaintance.

ADELE

Let's not discuss that, if you please; I begged you to come to speak of something else.

LEON

I am listening to you, Madame.

ADELE

For the last two months, sir, you've come here every day.

LEON

Not often enough, Madame.

ADELE

You must have noticed that you were received with pleasure.

LEON

I sometimes hoped so, Madame.

ADELE

The truth under which you presented yourself to me made it a duty to greet you this way. But doesn't it seem to you yourself that the time has come today to speak formally of your plans.

LEON

Oh! Madame, I am trembling.

ADELE

You!—young, possessing a distinguished estate, of a rich and honorable family—you can't fear a refusal.

LEON

Oh! Madame, are you saying what you think?

ADELE

What's more, I think I am saying what Pauline thinks.

LEON

Unfortunately, it's not a question of Pauline, Madame.

ADELE

What do you mean, sir?

LEON

When I came to your home and you willingly received me, I knew Miss Pauline and didn't know there could exist a woman who surpassed her in grace, in wit, in beauty. Then I saw you, Madame, and I had the joy of spending two months near you, and I was undeceived.

ADELE

Oh! What are you telling me?

LEON

It's because you are forcing me to it, Madame; as for me, first, I would never have dared to speak to you of my love, no, I would have locked it in my heart, and if you didn't read it in my eyes, divine it in the trembling of my voice, I would have kept you in ignorance of it. But I would at least be intoxicated with the pleasure of seeing you, with the joy of hearing you, I would have—

(De Vertpre half opens the door to hear better and then shuts it almost immediately from fear of being noticed. This action is repeated through the scene.)

ADELE

Shut up, sir, shut up!

LEON

Now, it's too late! This confession would be offensive without my telling you more. You spoke of my estate, of my family, of my fortune—you treat them as titles to the love of a woman. Well, my name, my estate, fortune—you will share all. I ask it on my knees—ah! You told me that I mustn't fear a refusal.

ADELE

But as for me, sir, I cannot—

LEON

Aren't you a widow? Aren't you free? Oh, your hand, your hand, darling!

ADELE

Sir, what have I done to deserve your forgetting yourself to such a degree?

LEON

I've not forgotten myself! To the contrary, I recollect.

ADELE

What?

LEON

It's a stupidity, perhaps—but I thought those slight services you were asking of me rather than someone else—I'd hoped that whole hours spent together, passed for both of us with a rapidity almost equal—some affectionate words—

ADELE

Oh! But sir—those slight services, those conversations, those affectionate words—all that—oh—all that was addressed to a friend.

LEON

It's a cruelty of someone of your age to choose friends of mine. The friend of a young and pretty woman must be at least sixty years old.

ADELE

You're joking, sir?

LEON

(falling to his knees) No, Madame, I am imploring.

ADELE

Ah! That's too much! Leave me alone—go away—go away.

LEON

I shan't withdraw without—

ADELE

Must I leave you the place?

LEON

I obey, Madame, but I hope that later—

ADELE

Never—

LEON

Oh, Madame—never—

ADELE

One more time—leave me, sir.

LEON

I am retiring.

(aside, leaving) Devil take me if I understand anything of this!

(He leaves. De Vertpre comes in. Adele is stupefied. They look at each other for a while without saying anything.)

De VERTPRE

Well, Madame?

ADELE

Well—sir, what do you want me to say?

De VERTPRE

Effectively, this young man was coming here for Pauline.

ADELE

Ah! Sir—be generous, I beg you.

De VERTPRE

Do you know it ended just in time. I heard plenty in that room—but I didn't see very well—and the way things were going—

ADELE

Mercy—I beg you.

De VERTPRE

Yes, you're right. It's not you I ought to be angry with—still, I am not sorry to get here.

ADELE

I am going to shut my door to this young man.

De VERTPRE

What folly! To make yourself an enemy—? No, no—

ADELE

What's your intention?

De VERTPRE

I will see him.

ADELE

A quarrel?

De VERTPRE

An explanation, that's all.

ADELE

And you will tell him?

De VERTPRE

Who I am.

ADELE

And your incognito?

De VERTPRE

I am renouncing it.

ADELE

But you are exposing yourself by giving it up.

De VERTPRE

I expose myself to nothing by keeping it, right?

ADELE

You can't think that a fool like that—

De VERTPRE

No—I don't think that; I prefer not to think that—at least—and after our discussion.

(starts to leave, but Adele retains him)

ADELE

My friend, I conjure you—

De VERTPRE

Listen, dear Adele—I didn't trouble your *tête-à-tête*—don't interfere with mine. That young man is in the garden—I am gong to join him.

ADELE

Paul—dear Paul.

De VERTPRE

Madame, to delay me further would make me believe that you

feared this interview still more for yourself than for me—that's not your intention, is it?

ADELE

No—surely not.

De VERTPRE

(gaily) Then, au revoir, dear angel.

(he goes out)

ADELE

(alone) What's he going to do? All that's needed is for one ironic word to insult the other. If I could see Leon, I would tell him to satisfy himself with friendship for me—that on that condition, I would forgive him for his mad behavior.

How could I think that these thousand nothings which form our relationship would encourage his love—? My God! What to do?

(crossing the stage) Ah! There's Leon on the garden, eyes fixed on this window—and my husband on this side looking for him. Leon's seen me! There he goes making signs to me! What presumption. He must think I'm calling. Why call him about all this? He doesn't seem to doubt it.

(making a sign with her head) Yes, yes, he's coming, the fool! And my husband, who's seen him and is running after him by the other alley—they will each take the opposite stairway, they'll meet here, and me between the two of them. Why, it's impossible! I'll go mad. There's Leon coming up running. I hear Paul's steps. What a ridiculous position. Here they are—my word! I'm getting out of here.

(she leaves)

(They each enter by opposite doors at the back.)

De VERTPRE

(drying his face) I got here in time.

LEON

Again, this gentleman! Ah, indeed, why, he does it furiously.

De VERTPRE

(breathless) Sir!

LEON

(breathless) Sir!

De VERTPRE

Were you running in the alley on the left?

LEON

And you in the alley on the right?

De VERTPRE

Myself.

LEON

I pay you my compliment. You have excellent legs.

De VERTPRE

Why, it seems to me yours don't refuse you service at all.

LEON

Tell me, without being indiscreet, will your business keep you here a long while?

De VERTPRE

And you, sir?

LEON

Oh! As for me, I'm almost living here.

De VERTPRE

And as for me, I'm going to live here right away.

LEON

In the home of Mme de Vertpre?

De VERTPRE

In the home of Mme de Vertpre? You'll excuse me.

(pulls a housecoat from his night sack) I am all well and—

LEON

What the devil are you doing then?

De VERTPRE

I am taking possession.

LEON

Of this room—?

De VERTPRE

Certainly.

LEON

But it adjoins that of Mme de Vertpre.

De VERTPRE

All the more reason.

LEON

And you are going to be in a bathrobe?

De VERTPRE

Indeed! I found you in your shirt.

LEON

Sir, I won't suffer—

De VERTPRE

Then you are more susceptible than I, because, as for me, I suffered.

LEON

Do you joke sometimes, sir—?

De VERTPRE

So as not to lose the habit—

LEON

And when this desire takes you, you attack?

De VERTPRE

Everybody—and give preference to my rivals, sir—

LEON

Meaning, sir—that you admit—

De VERTPRE

That I am your rival—? I have the impudence.

LEON

I needn't tell you I won't yield.

De VERTPRE

Any more than I!

LEON

Then I know a way—

De VERTPRE

I understand, I understand.

LEON

And you will adopt it?

De VERTPRE

I am not adopting it.

LEON

Sir!

De VERTPRE

Listen—what do we both want? To succeed, right? Well, if one of the two of us can reach his goal without killing the other—it seems to me that to be shown the door and receive a sword blow in the bargain would be a luxury.

LEON

So—we each go our own way?

De VERTPRE

We are going to do better.

LEON

I'm listening.

De VERTPRE

A proposal.

LEON

Speak, speak.

De VERTPRE

That the one of us who is least advanced in the good graces of Mme de Vertpre—it's of Mme de Vertpre you are amorous, right?

LEON

Yes, sir—

De VERTPRE

Very fine! Very fine! That the least advanced, I say, will cede his place to the other.

LEON

But who will keep faith?

De VERTPRE

You are a man of honor, I leave it up to you.

LEON

I thank you for your confidence, but I confess—

De VERTPRE

That you don't grant me yours. So be it! As for me, I will give proofs.

LEON

By Jove! That's too much.

De VERTPRE

You accept?

LEON

I accept.

De VERTPRE

And you will tell me everything?

LEON

(offering his hand) Word of honor.

De VERTPRE

(giving him a handshake) Come on—speak—and tell all.

LEON

(aside) Now, here's a passably stupid gentleman.

De VERTPRE

Well?

LEON

Well, sir—Mme de Vertpre, doubtless under the title of friend, having noticed that I don't like you and have much self-confidence—often accepts my services. On a walk, it's my arm she chooses in preference, a hand placed on an arm easily into another hand—and when this happens, by chance to the hand of Mme de Vertpre, our conversation preoccupies her enough so that she leaves it there—and more than once—

De VERTPRE

More than once?

LEON

I pressed it in mine without her thinking to withdraw it.

De VERTPRE

And so far, she didn't press yours?

LEON

No, sir, I must say it.

De VERTPRE

Well, I must tell you that as for me in a like circumstance, she pressed mine—and very tenderly still—

LEON

(surprised) Very tenderly?

De VERTPRE

So tenderly, that one day a ring that her husband gave her—

De VERTPRE

Mr. de Vertpre?

De VERTPRE

Mr. de Vertpre—remained in my hands.

LEON

And what did she do?

De VERTPRE

She left it there.

LEON

The proof.

De VERTPRE

(showing a ring) Here it is.

LEON

I indeed see a ring, but—

De VERTPRE

(opening the ring)

Looking—

LEON

(reading)

"Adele, Paul."

De VERTPRE

Are those indeed their baptismal names?

LEON

(a little disconcerted) I confess it, I am beaten.

De VERTPRE

To another!

LEON

Mme de Vertpre had her portrait made.

De VERTPRE

Ah! Ah!

LEON

A charming miniature, a perfect resemblance.

De VERTPRE

And so.

LEON

Well, Mme de Vertpre charged me with getting it from the painter, and when I returned it to her today, she asked me how I liked it, in a manner to make me think—

De VERTPRE

What?

LEON

That she wouldn't be slow to offer it to the person it is destined for.

De VERTPRE

And this person?

LEON

Tomorrow's my birthday, sir—

De VERTPRE

And mine today; you see she wanted me to have it.

(shows him the portrait)

LEON

(completely surprised) Ah!

De VERTPRE

Continue, sir—

LEON

My word—if that's the way it is, I am going to tell you everything.

De VERTPRE

(wiping his face) I am prepared.

LEON

Mme de Vertpre loves readings—often, at night, when the door is shut to everybody, after Pauline is retired, we would choose, in the library, some poems of André Chanier or Lamartine. We would open some novel by Nadier or by Victor Hugo—and it was the most tender page, the most delirious verse we sought. When the book was shut, our words succeeded those of the great authors; and they preserved, if not the talent, at least the tincture of their words—thus the time, so long for others, the time passed, time flew from us and—

De VERTPRE

And what? Do me the pleasure of finishing.

LEON

Midnight sounds.

De VERTPRE

Midnight sounds—

LEON

We promised each other for the next day as sweet a night, and

I retired—

De VERTPRE

Well, as for me, sir, it's exactly the same except—

LEON

Except what?

De VERTPRE

Except that I remained.

LEON

(getting hot) Sir, that's an infamous slander, and you will give me satisfaction for the insult you are doing to the purest of women.

De VERTPRE

Very fine, young man!

LEON

And wonder who, rare amongst all, has never in her life had a thought capable of being reproached—even in her dream.

De VERTPRE

Bravo!

LEON

Of the only woman for whose honor I would answer for with

my life.

De VERTPRE

Allow me to embrace you.

LEON

(repulsing him) Oh! Don't jest, sir! You've offered me proofs. Well, I demand them instantly, this minute.

De VERTPRE

The Devil! But such proofs are difficult to furnish.

LEON

I warn you that I must have them, sir—

De VERTPRE

A letter.

LEON

Perhaps forged and besides, I don't know her writing—I don't think, I boasted, she wrote me—something else, sir—something else—!

De VERTPRE

Ah—by Jove—

(pulling the portrait from his pocket)

LEON

Well? Her portrait. I've already seen it.

De VERTPRE

Push this little spring.

LEON

Sir, this portrait doesn't prove a thing.

De VERTPRE

Push!

LEON

(stupefied) Yours.

De VERTPRE

Read!

LEON

"Given by my Adele, June 28th, 1825—the day of our marriage."

De VERTPRE

You find it resembling?

LEON

This painting is devilishly flattering to you, sir—

De VERTPRE

Still, you recognized me right away.

LEON

Then your name is—?

De VERTPRE

Paul de Vertpre.

LEON

And you are not dead?

De VERTPRE

See if I am imposing.

LEON

So—the rumor that was spread.

De VERTPRE

Was necessitated by circumstances.

LEON

And Mme de Vertpre knew you were living?

De VERTPRE

I never allowed her to forget it, I beg you to believe.

LEON

Then she was making fun of me?

De VERTPRE

(laughing) Why—I'm afraid so—

LEON

That's fine. I will avenge myself.

De VERTPRE

(uneasily) How's that?

LEON

I know what to do.

De VERTPRE

Huh?

LEON

The whole world will think I'm right.

De VERTPRE

Not at all, sir, the whole world will consider you wrong.

LEON

Little mater to me.

De VERTPRE

You'll be wasting your time.

LEON

I am young.

De VERTPRE

You will get tired.

LEON

I have patience.

De VERTPRE

But this is bull-headedness. As for me, sir—I haven't done anything to you.

LEON

So I wish you no ill.

De VERTPRE

That's indeed lucky.

LEON

No—you are a brave man! It's your wife I intend to avenge myself on—

De VERTPRE

Take care, Mr. Lawyer, we are married under a community property regime.

LEON

That's all the same to me.

De VERTPRE

But it's not to me.

LEON

So much the worse!

De VERTPRE

Ah indeed—you're crazy!

LEON

No, sir, I am burned. One has a reputation as a young man.

De VERTPRE

And so?

LEON

And one has to keep it.

De VERTPRE

And as for me, sir, my reputation as a husband—do you think I intend to ruin it?

LEON

It's not that I love her, at least—your wife!

De VERTPRE

And you are right.

LEON

I detest her.

De VERTPRE

Right.

LEON

But it's all the same to me—I will sacrifice myself!

De VERTPRE

You are too good.

LEON

A coquette.

De VERTPRE

Ah! Yes—for goodness sake.

LEON

Who thinks herself pretty.

De VERTPRE

And who isn't?

LEON

Yes, sir—she is—you haven't come to teach me—but a character.

De VERTPRE

Atrocious!

LEON

Why, it's because she thinks I love her.

De VERTPRE

Why the devil did you tell her so?

LEON

I lied! It's Pauline that I love—what a difference between the two—! Pauline, so pure, so sweet, so naive—who would weep in advance at the very idea of causing me shame! Pauline—that she could think I had forgotten her—! Oh—she will know that I didn't love her for a minute—she will know it!

De VERTPRE

Right away, right away—

LEON

Yes, sir—much later.

De VERTPRE

And, meanwhile, you will allow her to enjoy her conquest, to boast of keeping you near her like a child—it will give Pauline time to notice your indifference and to love another for it.

LEON

You're right, she will be very proud.

De VERTPRE

Listen: better than that.

LEON

What can be done?

De VERTPRE

Wait, I've only known you an instant, but you are good, you have a candid soul, you are an excellent young man, and I love you like a brother.

LEON

Thanks—

De VERTPRE

I am joining you against my wife.

LEON

Let's see.

De VERTPRE

In your place, here's what I would do.

LEON

Speak.

De VERTPRE

I would ask Mme de Vertpre for an interview.

LEON

I'd really like that.

De VERTPRE

With her husband present, it would be all the same to me.

LEON

No—I'd prefer that it be alone.

De VERTPRE

Well, alone, that's all the same to me—and I would tell her that what I'd done was only a game so I could make fun of her—that I had never loved her—that I never could love her—that it is Pauline alone—follow carefully what I am telling you—that it's Pauline alone that I love—and the proof is that I am demanding her as my wife.

LEON

Suppose she refuses her to me?

De VERTPRE

As for me, I will give her to you.

LEON

Allow me to ponder—

De VERTPRE

No—look, these things must be done immediately, carried off in a moment of rage, because one puts it over a widow, a real one who doesn't suspect the frankness of feelings. Pauline is a charming child, you are going to see.

(rings)

(Helene appears.)

De VERTPRE

Helene, tell Pauline that her uncle isn't dead; that he's come, and she should come.

(Helene leaves.)

De VERTPRE

I'm going to make myself known to her; I will tell her your intentions.

PAULINE

(enters very joyous) Oh, my uncle, my good uncle—I've learned you are not dead—how happy I am; I am very satisfied.

De VERTPRE

And me too—I am satisfied and happy and I am not alone.

PAULINE

What do you mean?

De VERTPRE

Here—here's Leon, who is in a dilemma.

(to Leon) Pull yourself together, Leon—it's decided—nothing prevents your happiness.

PAULINE

What are you saying, uncle?

De VERTPRE

I say that this young man adores you.

PAULINE

And as for me, I detest him.

De VERTPRE

What are you talking about? A love so pure, so ardent! Why say something like that? What were you telling me just now, Leon?

LEON

That I love Miss—

De VERTPRE

That you love her? You said that you were mad, that you couldn't live without her—that you'd blow out your brains if your didn't obtain her. That's almost what you said, right?

LEON

Not at all, but—

De VERTPRE

Do you hear? He was repeating that he'd blow out his brains—unhappy young man—a suicide—could you really be thinking of it?

PAULINE

What, Leon—you love me to such a degree?

LEON

Oh—more than you can imagine.

De VERTPRE

And he added—"I wish she were there so I could fall at her feet."

(to Leon) On your knees.

(to Pauline) The only happiness for him must be obtained from your mouth.

(to Leon) On your knees.

(to Pauline) The admission is paid by the return. And you cannot refuse him, for it's a true love, that sees, that feels—and you will answer for his death.

(to Leon) Will you get on your knees?

(Leon falls to his knees.)

PAULINE

Ah—if I thought it was true!

LEON

Believe it, for your uncle is telling you the complete truth, and as for me, I still have a thousand things, a thousand things to tell you.

PAULINE

And as for me, Leon, I have only one.

LEON

Say it then.

PAULINE

I love you.

De VERTPRE

(solemnly) Children.

(grasping their hands) I join you together.

(aside) This wasn't easy.

PAULINE

(to de Vertpre) Uncle, only my aunt can dispose of my hand, she is my second mother, and I will belong only to the man of her choice.

De VERTPRE

That's very fine; tell her all this, and as for us, we are going to find the notary.

LEON

Ah, leave us alone together.

De VERTPRE

No, no, you see things like these must be finished at one sitting.

(aside) No telling what might happen.

(taking Leon aside) And now, my nephew, you are half avenged.

(aloud) It remains for you to ask Pauline's hand of her aunt and to tell her—you know what you have to tell her—the rest.

LEON

Don't worry—goodbye, darling Pauline—I am leaving you but to occupy myself about our happiness—and to hasten it as much as possible.

PAULINE

You will never return quickly enough.

(Exit Leon and De Vertpre.)

PAULINE

Oh—my God! My God! How happy I am! Who would have believed this? My uncle is good enough not to be dead, and has just returned from the United States to marry me to—Leon, who loves me—who loves only me—those black looks were not true—it's I who am—that poor lad who was soaked—soaked.

ADELE

(entering hurriedly) Where are they?

PAULINE

They went out together.

ADELE

Great God! They must be prevented.

PAULINE

No, auntie, don't stop them.

ADELE

But, unhappy girl—they are going to fight!

PAULINE

At the notaries?

ADELE

What do you mean?

PAULINE

They are going to find him for my marriage contract.

ADELE

They weren't quarreling when they went out?

PAULINE

They were talking like old friends.

ADELE

Really!

PAULINE

And I am really satisfied! Leon—

ADELE

Really seems like a fool to me, my dear child.

PAULINE

Not at all, auntie. He adores me—I assure you he's in his right mind completely.

ADELE

I mean to say that he gives me the impression of a scatterbrain.

PAULINE

I don't know, but he swore to me that he loved only me—and that he'd never loved anyone but me. Is that being scatterbrained, auntie?

ADELE

And where did he take this oath to you?

PAULINE

Here—at my knees.

ADELE

Poor child!

ADELE

Perhaps I should tell her that he was at my knees an hour ago—oh, no, why affect her with a folly?

PAULINE

What are you thinking about, auntie?

ADELE

About what you've just told me. And you've engaged your hand?

PAULINE

My hand? That's for you to dispose of, and I said that to uncle and Leon.

ADELE

So indeed—Leon?

PAULINE

Is going to come ask you for it.

ADELE

In league with my husband?

PAULINE

Very much in league; it's my uncle who is prompting him.

ADELE

And Mr. de Vertpre is no longer dead for Leon or for you?

PAULINE

Very much alive for both of us.

ADELE

I'd really like to have a pen and ink.

PAULINE

Would you like me to ring?

ADELE

No—go find them in my room.

PAULINE

You are going to write him?

ADELE

Don't be concerned.

(Pauline leaves.)

ADELE

Ah, gentleman, it seems there's a conspiracy and that you understand each other marvelously. My husband, I conceive that he hurries this marriage—but Leon, who was just now—that young man needs a lesson and he's not going to escape it—and if he really wants to marry Pauline—

And I was forgetting my husband! That's unjust! He also deserves a punishment for his jealousy—he shall have it.

PAULINE

(returning with writing materials which she places on the table) Here, auntie? What are you going to do?

ADELE

Listen, Pauline—it's a serious matter when a link that binds us for all our life is given to another—when a link that only death can break once men have formed it.

PAULINE

Oh! Yes—it's a celestial happiness.

ADELE

Or an eternal misfortune.

PAULINE

What do you mean?

ADELE

Well, Pauline, we mustn't deliver to chance all the hopes of your youth. We enter into life with happy, laughing years; don't shorten them, dear child.

PAULINE

You frighten me! Do you refuse to consent to my marriage?

ADELE

No, no—but first and foremost I want to perform a test.

PAULINE

On Leon?

ADELE

On Leon. Will you place everything in my hands?

PAULINE

Hasn't all you've done until now been for my happiness?

ADELE

I intend to continue. He doesn't know your handwriting?

PAULINE

No.

ADELE

Nor mine. Well! Sit there and write.

PAULINE

I obey.

ADELE

(hesitating) "Remaining alone after you left. I was almost remorseful of the way in which I first received the confession of a love that seemed so real and so passionate."

PAULINE

It's true, auntie—for I told him I detested him.

ADELE

(dictating) "But that's the way it is with the heart of a woman. Rarely is it permitted to express all it feels—it's necessary, when one is a man to pity and pardon."

PAULINE

I understand the ending much less.

ADELE

(smiling) Oh—that doesn't matter. Give me the letter and go wait for me in my apartment.

PAULINE

How much time will you need for your test?

(Sitting at the table Pauline has vacated and hiding the letter.)

ADELE

A quarter of an hour.

PAULINE

(aside) Good! I'll return in ten minutes.

(she leaves)

ADELE

Just in time, here's Leon.

LEON

(enters, speaking to de Vertpre) Don't worry, my dear uncle, I know what I have to say.

ADELE

(aside) And so do I!

(She rises seemingly troubled, clasping the letter in her hand.)

LEON

(turning aside) Mme de Vertpre.

(aloud) Excuse me for entering like this, Madame. But I thought you were in your room. Anyway, I was with your husband—that's my excuse.

ADELE

You were thinking to find another person here, weren't you?

LEON

No—it's you I was looking for, Madame—Madame—

(aside) The Devil—it's more difficult to begin than I thought.

(aloud) You must have found me very stupid and really ridiculous?

ADELE

I found you very imprudent at least—

LEON

And you've indeed punished my imprudence. I thank you for it, Madame; in desperate illnesses, violent remedies must be employed; I suffered, but I've been cured.

ADELE

I congratulate myself, sir, for having effectuated such a marvelous cure, and especially one so prompt.

LEON

Your severity, Madame, left me no hope.

ADELE

Was I so severe?

LEON

Why—except for having me put out the door by your people, I don't see much more.

ADELE

You are unaware of the position I was in—and that my husband was hidden in this room, listening to our conversation and obliging me to use prudence.

LEON

(astonished) Mr. de Vertpre was there? Ah! As I was saying, Mme de Vertpre, that this severity—for you were very severe—enlightened me as to my true feelings. My wounded vanity made me see clearly into my own heart.

    Yes—I was fascinated, seduced by the charm of your conversation—because I know what attracts eyes and minds to you. But this feeling was superficial, it left the depth of my heart intact, while the love that I had for Pauline—and when you took pity on my folly, it vanished like a dream never to return.

ADELE

Now that's the second confession you made me today, sir—the second is at least as strange as the first—and perhaps the moment is yet even more ill chosen to do it.

LEON

What are you saying?

ADELE

I am saying, sir—that if you are not indeed an egoist, you are at least superficial.

LEON

Me, Madame?

ADELE

How good it is for oneself to play with such feelings when one is severe ridding oneself of them as soon as they present themselves to us—or rejecting them at our will like a grief that leaves us—but I will add that God hasn't given all the creatures that left his hands your philosophy and your strength.

(She turns away to smile. The same action occurs throughout the scene.)

LEON

I ask your pardon, Madame, but—

ADELE

And if—instead of following your example, the woman to whom you were addressing yourself to play this game took seriously that which seemed only a jest to you—if she was unable to distinguish in your tender eyes fixed on her—in your trembling voice, when you were speaking to her—this act of an actor which in you makes the false so perfectly resemble the truth. If—frank and naive, she had let her heart abandon itself to all these hopes of a love which was being born; if each day had added to her hopes; if this love—the love of a woman slid into all her being, seized all her life, if it had become her cult, her only god in this world, and then you came to tell her—her—what you just confessed to me—to me! Oh! Say, sir—wouldn't she go mad from it and die of it?

LEON

(in the last embarrassment) Oh but—that's not—Madame!

ADELE

That could be, sir—

LEON

You really have me frightened with this joke.

ADELE

Did I joke? I thought to have suffered. Pardon, I was mistaken.

LEON

But Madame, these reproaches that you are making me, Pauline could also make them to me.

ADELE

I know it. Do you think, sir, that would make you more excusable?

LEON

Why, Madame, you are saying too much or too little.

ADELE

(feigning the greatest trouble) This letter ought to have been delivered to you when I met you here—it will speak more clearly than I can do.

(tendering him the letter)

LEON

(hesitating) A letter?

ADELE

And will you refuse to read it?

LEON

(taking it) Refuse? No, no—on the contrary, I am indeed happy to.

ADELE

Say, really cruel!

(she leaves laughing stealthily)

LEON

(falling overwhelmed into an armchair) Yes, the fact is I've been indeed cruel and without suspecting it—may God forgive me! Here I am between two loves like these. There just wasn't a way to tell her a word about my marriage. A letter?

(looking at it with terror) Why, it's because I don't love her anymore at all; as for me, I don't know how this is managed. A letter—come on—some courage. We must read it. "Left alone after you left—I almost felt remorse for the manner in which I had just received the confession of a love which seemed so true and so impassioned." Oh, there's not doubt!
Let's continue.

(wiping his face) "But that's the way it is with a woman's heart. Rarely is it permitted to express all that it feels." I hope that's clear—that! "When one is a man, one must pity and forgive." Yes, certainly, I pity myself but I don't forgive myself.

(falling back in the chair) It's even more unfortunate! Why, it's fatality! Oh women! Women! It's terrible when you think about it. Mme de Vertpre—to betray her husband—a charming man, full of wit—of frankness—as young as I am—for he's not forty years old yet—and I am more than twenty.
And for whom? For—certainly, it's flattering for me—never mind—I mustn't permit it. But what to do?

(rising excitedly) My uncle is going to come ask me the result; the result is pretty—still, as for me, I cannot tell him—I prefer he learn it from someone else and my faith!

(going to escape through the door at the left and stopping) Ah, there he is below on the terrace. If I go down by this door, or the other—he's going to see me—is there no way for me to escape? This way! Ah, yes—it's Pauline's apartment—what I will tell him if I meet him? This door—it leads to Mme de Vertpre. Ah, indeed, why I am cornered?—ah, this window, which gives on the garden—a bit high—but my word, it's on the grass.

(as he climbs the window, Vertpre enters softly and seeing him ready to jump, stops him by the end of his clothes, they both look at each other)

De VERTPRE

What the devil are you doing there?

LEON

(coming from the window) Me, nothing, uncle, I am taking the air!

De VERTPRE

Well—the interview?

LEON

(aside) Ah, yes, the interview. Now we are there.

De VERTPRE

The scene was very hot?

LEON

Very hot.

De VERTPRE

Tell me about it.

LEON

Uncle, let go of me.

De VERTPRE

What!

LEON

I beg you. You won't be angry.

De VERTPRE

Not at all.

LEON

You want me to remain?

De VERTPRE

I insist on it.

LEON

(aside) One cannot flee one's destiny.

De VERTPRE

You were saying?

LEON

My poor uncle!

De VERTPRE

Huh?

LEON

You cause me much pain.

De VERTPRE

Huh?

LEON

For indeed you are good—you deserve to be loved.

De VERTPRE

Come on, come on, indeed.

LEON

Why don't you see what the thing is that embarrasses me?

De VERTPRE

What's that supposed to mean? Did Pauline refuse you?

LEON

By Jove.

De VERTPRE

What do you mean, 'By Jove'? Now there's a 'By Jove' that's really bizarre.

LEON

But frankly, can she give it to me? Such sacrifices are beyond the strength of a woman.

De VERTPRE

Come on—when are you going to explain yourself?

LEON

Why, you still don't understand me?

De VERTPRE

What?

LEON

You still don't understand that your wife—? Why, it's very difficult to tell a husband these things, and you ought to spare me the annoyance. No? Well, uncle, your wife's in love with me, that's all.

De VERTPRE

Ah! That's all? Ah, indeed! But you are—I hope—lunatic.

LEON

No, uncle—I am—I am very mortified.

De VERTPRE

And as for me! It seems to me! But this morning I heard—I was there.

LEON

Well, that's just it. This morning you were there—and she knew you were there—tonight, you are no longer there, and she knew you are no longer there.

De VERTPRE

(with a stupid look) Bah!

LEON

It's your fault, uncle—it's you who are the cause of all this. Has anyone ever been seen to pass himself off as dead? I ask if there exists in this world circumstances capable of making a husband adopt such a resolution? But tell me what forced you to do it?

De VERTPRE

Yes, the moment is really well chosen to tell you this tale, isn't it?

LEON

It's you who got us where we are. You wanted me to have an interview with your wife—well—I had that interview and I forgive you.

De VERTPRE

He forgives me! Well, he's really excellent, he is!

LEON

Yes—because you couldn't guess the outcome.

You couldn't possibly think she would give me to understand so clearly—

De VERTPRE

She gave you to understand clearly—?

LEON

Oh—if this had stopped there, there would still be way to elude it—

De VERTPRE

Ah—it didn't stop there?

LEON

No, no, uncle, it went much further.

De VERTPRE

Tell me quickly where it went.

LEON

Perhaps I ought not to—for a man of honor must keep such secrets—if not for himself—at least for the woman who confided them to him. But—

De VERTPRE

But we gave each other our word to tell each other.

LEON

I know it—and it's that promise which made me prefer to leave by the window.

De VERTPRE

Young man—in the name of that word which I myself respected—because I told you everything—in the name of honor, I adjure you—

LEON

You recall, uncle—this morning I was telling you that I didn't know the handwriting of your wife?

De VERTPRE

Well?

LEON

Well—tonight, I know it.

De VERTPRE

She wrote you?

LEON

She's written me.

De VERTPRE

That can't be.

LEON

That can't be? That's extraordinary—they are all like that.

De VERTPRE

You say that to frighten me. It's a joke. Come on, come on—it's a joke, right?

LEON

Yes, I'm really in a mood to joke! You deserve for me to show you this letter.

De VERTPRE

I defy you to do so!

LEON

(pointing to his left hand in which he holds it) Well, uncle, here, I cannot let you read it—but there it is.

De VERTPRE

(coming forward to take it) There it is. Leon, in the name of your uncle's honor that's been so gravely compromised—because it is gravely compromised—the honor of your uncle—you don't doubt it?

LEON

No, uncle—I don't doubt it.

De VERTPRE

Deliver that letter to me, I beg you.

LEON

Impossible!

De VERTPRE

Why, then, it contains things—

LEON

It contains them.

De VERTPRE

Worse than what you've told me?

LEON

Oh! No—

De VERTPRE

Well?

LEON

Why, a letter, uncle, is a proof; is it for me to give it to you?

De VERTPRE

I will return it to you. Word of honor.

(grabbing it away) I have it.

LEON

Oh—uncle—uncle—

De VERTPRE

Leave me alone. I will be prudent. What am I about to read.

(collapses annihilated in an armchair)

LEON

(speaking to himself) What an odd thing! I ask you—to await the return of her husband when seeing me every day privately, it was so easy for her—

De VERTPRE

(rising, excited) And what is it you're saying there?

LEON

Pardon! Pardon! Why, I am desperate—for still if she refuses Pauline to me—

De VERTPRE

Pauline? You are thinking of getting married with my example before your eyes—? No, no—I won't allow it.

LEON

Uncle, uncle! If you exasperate me—I am capable of anything. I warn you.

De VERTPRE

Young man, young man! Leon, my nephew—do you want to make me die? Don't you see I am beside myself, that—I don't know what I'm saying?

LEON

Ah—it's true! Poor uncle! Pardon! Pardon!

De VERTPRE

Ah!

(they throw themselves in each other's arms. They embrace several times) Come on, courage!

(opening the letter with the greatest agitation—then as he reads, his face becomes laughing) Pauline's handwriting! What's this signify? You are sure it was my wife who delivered this letter to you?

LEON

He doubts it.

De VERTPRE

Then I understand.

LEON

Poor man, he understands! That's horrifying.

(de Vertpre laughs.)

LEON

In what a state of agitation he is!

(de Vertpre crosses the stage.)

LEON

What's he going to do? Where's he going to go? Uncle, I beg you—do nothing imprudent—

De VERTPRE

Don't worry.

LEON

This letter. At least return this letter to me.

De VERTPRE

I will return it to you before my wife.

(Adele appears with Pauline in the doorway of her apartment.)

ADELE

We are here.

LEON

The two of you were listening?

De VERTPRE

(going to his wife and leading her forward by the arm) Madame, henceforth when Pauline writes letters, beg her to sign them—and you will spare me one of the most chagrining scenes I've ever had in my life.

ADELE

That will teach you to be jealous.

De VERTPRE

Me, jealous? How can you say that? Pauline.

(giving her the letter) Return this to the gentleman—

LEON

What—this letter—

PAULINE

Is from me! Are you angry, sir, with what I wrote?

LEON

Oh!

(to Adele) So, Madame, you don't love me?

ADELE

(gaily) Not the least in the world, sir—but I owed a lesson to a heedless person.

LEON

Oh—how I thank you! But this scene.

ADELE

Didn't you yourself tell me that the reproaches I was making you, Pauline could make as well. I was her agent.

LEON

Ah! Can I at least hope?

ADELE

You don't deserve it, still.

(looking at Pauline) We would like to believe that you weren't lying when this morning you told her you never loved me and you only loved her—

LEON

And Pauline.

ADELE

Belongs to you.

De VERTPRE

She belongs to you, my nephew. And to say that none of all this would have happened but for the necessity which make me pass for dead.

LEON

Ah! Now I hope you are going to tell us the reason.

De VERTPRE

Nothing more fair. Imagine—

(all listening)

HELENE

Sir, it's the notary and the contract.

De VERTPRE

I'll tell you about it tomorrow.

CURTAIN

PORTHOS IN SEARCH OF AN OUTFIT: A COMEDY IN ONE ACT

by Auguste Anicet-Bourgeois, Philippe Dumanoir, and Édouard Brisebarre

For Harry Hayfield

CAST OF CHARACTERS

Porthos, a musketeer

Coquenard, a solicitor

Jupin, a furrier

Biquet, Coquenard's Clerk

Ursula, Wife of Coquenard

Philomela, wife of Jupin

The play takes place in Paris in the reign of Louis XIII

PORTHOS IN SEARCH OF AN OUTFIT

The stage represents an office furnished severely and in the style of the sixteenth century. To the left, a large transept window further back, doors left and right and at the far back. To the right, a small desk covered with papers. A large chimney to the right—to the left near the back door, a buffet—to the right, a table, chairs, pigeon holes, etc.

COQUENARD

(outside) Biquet! Biquet!

BIQUET

(outside) Boss?

COQUENARD

(entering from the right, with a worried air, shouting) Noon—the stroke of noon by all the clocks in the quarter—she hasn't yet returned from Saint Mercy, our parish. I must be red with worry.

JUPIN

(entering from the left, looking all around) Not a human shape.

(noticing Coquenard) Ah!

(going to him) Old friend, Coquenard.

COQUENARD

Pal Jupin.

JUPIN

The most powerful solicitor of the Rue Brise-Miche.

COQUENARD

The greatest furrier of the Rue Ours.

(shouting very loud) Biquet!

BIQUET

(who is standing behind him, very calmly) Right here, boss.

COQUENARD

(pointing him out to Jupin) My first clerk. I have only this one.

(to Biquet) Run quickly to Saint Mercy—find her—even in the organ loft—and bring her to me.

BIQUET

Who's that?

COQUENARD

(pushing him quickly outside) Madame Coquenard, my wife,

my better half—big mouth.

JUPIN

His better half—he's got a—what! I take a little trip to Auvergne to direct my harvest of chestnuts. I leave you a bachelor, and I return to find you married and—

COQUENARD

Not yet, Jupin.

(with abandon) There comes a time, you see, when one feels the need to have a companion at your side.

JUPIN

And you've got married?

COQUENARD

Twenty years old—some money—and attractive.

JUPIN

(shaking his head) Twenty years old—the devil!

COQUENARD

(singing) Charming age—the beautiful years of my wife—have suddenly warmed my winter. I am bursting into bloom—my soul is green again—yes—it's marriage that's rejuvenated me, my dear boy—

JUPIN

(singing) Oh, rejuvenated.

COQUENARD

(singing) Consider—it's quite clear—alone, I'm forty. The innocent child has seen only twenty springs. Since added up the two of us are sixty, my half is only thirty. Lucky rogue—I'm just thirty again.

JUPIN

Anyway—this wife.

COQUENARD

A penitent of the Convent of the Visitation—whose only relative, an old female cousin—my client—made me her tutor before her decease.

JUPIN

Understood.

COQUENARD

The poor little darling was bored at La Visitation—which the deceased had ordered that she never leave except to enter the control of a husband—but be it luck, be it fate—not one suitor appeared—and so my pupil wouldn't expire of languishing. I sacrificed myself—I gave her my hand.

JUPIN

(with malice) In exchange for the inheritance of the old relative.

COQUENARD

(sighing) Half of which will return to a little male cousin—that no one's been able to discover yet, despite every effort—that I propose to make.

JUPIN

Pooh—perhaps he's dead.

COQUENARD

I am delighted by that thought. I don't wish him ill—but I quite sincerely wish him that indisposition.

(with good humor) Not for myself, my God! But for my wife—who has a taste for economy—that I am developing—and whose only violent passion is—

JUPIN

—for you?

COQUENARD

(giving himself airs) First of all—and for a spaniel that I gave her—he's her little cavalier.

JUPIN

As that of Madame Jupin.

(sighing) Who is still the woman most on horseback.

COQUENARD

Bah!

JUPIN

Of virtue. She's fasting now—14 times a week—twice a day—

COQUENARD

That regime would aggravate my constitution.

JUPIN

What do you want—she makes me so happy in other ways—she is so good to others. Heavens, even while I was in Auvergne, she sheltered on the recommendation of her director a kind of mercenary—our distant cousin who had fenced—despite the prohibitions of Milord Cardinal Richelieu and the hardened soldier disappeared without paying his bill of 200 pistoles—for value received in furnishings—

(giving him a paper) She—rather—

COQUENARD

(taking it and reading) Eh—eh—eh—Porthos, Musketeers of His Majesty Louis XIII.

JUPIN

Philomela wants you to collect it.

COQUENARD

I will.

JUPIN

So he's lodged at the Petit-Chalet.

COQUENARD

I will find lodging for him there.

(places the note on his desk)

URSULA

(outside—weeping) Ah, my God! My God!

COQUENARD

Who is it crying like that?

BIQUET

(running in from the back) It's your wife, boss—that I just met on the Rue St. Martin returning from the parish.

(he leaves after the couplet sung by Ursula)

URSULA

(singing) My poor Mimi.
My sweet friend.
My so cherished companion.
When you were ravished from me
I'm left with nothing
Except my husband.

JUPIN

(low to Coquenard) I compliment you.

COQUENARD

(singing) As for me, my dear, I'm losing my wits.

JUPIN

It's just that she's charming!

COQUENARD

(singing) She's better when she laughs.

URSULA

My poor Mimi.

(singing) My—

(noticing Jupin) (spoken) Some one!

(the orchestra stops playing)

COQUENARD

Jupin—our friend—of whom I've spoken to you—but what has happened to you?

URSULA

Alas—I lost my Mimi!

JUPIN

The devil!

(reflecting to Coquenard) What exactly is her Mimi—?

COQUENARD

It's a name that I gave—

URSULA

—To my spaniel, sir.

JUPIN

(aside) Is that dumb—to give to an animal like that the name of Mimi.

(aloud) I call my wife's—Lola—

(aside) Well and good!

URSULA

He was at my side. The service terminated, I got up—and the red ribbon to which he was attached was no longer in my hand—

COQUENARD

And the dog—

URSULA

Even less!

COQUENARD

I suspected so!

URSULA

I look, I call, I ask around—useless, my God! No one had seen him.

(weeping) Dear Mimi, hoo, hoo, hoo—

COQUENARD

(aside) Why that comedian there is doing me wrong—I am not sorry that he's lost.

(aloud) Come on, Ursula, console yourself—pretty one—there are still dogs in the world—right Jupin?

JUPIN

Certainly—I know some—

COQUENARD

If we don't find Mimi—eh! Well—

(with effort) I will make a sacrifice—I will buy you a poodle or a bulldog much bigger—less easy to lose—come Jupin we'll go run after the ingrate.

(to Ursula) Come on, stop—if you keep on crying, I won't hug you.

(Ursula cries all the more.)

URSULA

(to Coquenard) What innocence, huh? She's a treasure I'm guarding.

JUPIN

(aside) Like his money—without spending it.

COQUENARD

Till later, honey—we will return with Mimi—or with another—that will do tricks—who will give his paw—give me your arm, Jupin.

(he leaves by the rear taking Jupin along)

URSULA

(alone) Another than Mimi—I only want him—what do I care about others? Mr. Coquenard will not find him I am sure of it. He's so clumsy.

(desolate) I will never see him again.

(considering) At least so long as he doesn't discover him—that young man who for the last several days was to be found on my way endlessly—at church—and who saw my tears and my despair—he threw himself under the portico shouting to me that he would bring him back dead or alive—brave young man—he never failed to be at the services at which I was present—that's really having piety at the same time as me—

I hope indeed that he succeeds—it seems to me that I would love him for having brought Mimi back to me—and that I will love Mimi even more because it's he who brought him to me.

BIQUET

(outside) The boss forbids anyone to speak to the lady when he's not here.

PORTHOS

(outside) Out of the way, kid.
Little limb of the law!

URSULA

(terrified) Oh, my God!

BIQUET

You'll only enter by passing over my dead body!

PORTHOS

(outside) Well—I will pass over it.

BIQUET

(rolls through the door at back) Mercy!

PORTHOS

(stepping over him) Didn't I tell you I would pass over it?

URSULA

(aside) What do I see—him!

PORTHOS

Her!

URSULA

That uproar—what is the cause?

PORTHOS

(advancing gallantly) Don't worry, Madame—he's an animal.

BIQUET

(indignant) Me, an animal!

PORTHOS

No, not you—an different one—more intelligent, more beautiful.

URSULA

(excited) My spaniel.

PORTHOS

Who I had the luck to grab by the collar—and but for this imbecile

(to Biquet) It's of you I am speaking this time.

(to Ursula) I would have brought him in person to implore his pardon.

(singing) To your tender weeping.

To your good sweet caress.
I bring the lost sheep.
Mimi returns to your knees.

(reaction by Ursula)

Can I look on without irritation
When a spaniel breaks a chain.
That so many men would like to wear!

URSULA

(naively) You want to wear his collar?

PORTHOS

Figuratively—let's understand each other.
    Mimi has taken a time to run about towards his kennel or his dog food.

URSULA

Biquet—go quick, give him his pâté—

BIQUET

Excuse me! A solicitor's first clerk—who—

PORTHOS

(threatening him) To that pâté, Biquet!

(pushes him violently and makes him leave by the rear)

URSULA

(at the peak of joy) Ah! Sir—I don't know what to say. What to do—to thank you for what I owe you.

PORTHOS

Pretty women don't owe me a thing—ever—on the contrary, it's I who—and I always acquit myself.

URSULA

(naively) Pretty—me? That's singular—my husband never told me that—

PORTHOS

There are indeed many things that he probably never told you— we will busy ourselves with them.

URSULA

(wanting to get away) Thanks, sir, thanks! Okay—I will never forget you—

PORTHOS

(stopping her) You are leaving me—?

URSULA

My husband has told me never to talk with a man other than him—

PORTHOS

(to himself) Why he brought her up very badly.

(aloud) Stay at least until I have obtained the honest reward that is my due—a kiss—oh—only one.

URSULA

Come back tomorrow, sir—I will ask permission of my husband today.

PORTHOS

I grant you that—fear nothing I will take it all on myself—

URSULA

That's different—then kiss me, sir—it no longer concerns me anymore!

(they embrace several times)

COQUENARD

(entering from the back, aside) Bulldogs are way over priced—I will buy her a starling.

(aloud) Great God!

URSULA

Mr. Coquenard.

PORTHOS

The husband!

COQUENARD

On the cheek.

PORTHOS

No—on both.

(kissing Ursula) Like that, see—

COQUENARD

(furious) Jesus!

PORTHOS

Now—it's your turn.

(he grabs him and drags him) Don't budge.

COQUENARD

(trying to free himself) Will you indeed finish?—Who is this man here?

(furious) Who are you, stranger?

PORTHOS

(embarrassed) Who am I—solicitor?

(gaily) Hey—I am—me—

COQUENARD

Is it possible?

PORTHOS

Word of honor—let's hug again.

COQUENARD

With all my heart.

(pushing away, and considering) But who—are you?

URSULA

(aside) He intends to deceive my husband.

PORTHOS

(embarrassed) I am—

URSULA

(whispering low) My cousin.

PORTHOS

The cousin of your wife. Your wife's cousin.

COQUENARD

(explosively) I suspected it.

PORTHOS

(aside) Not me!

COQUENARD

Consequently your name is—

PORTHOS

(embarrassed) Yes—

URSULA

(whispering to him) Hercule de Bouillancour!

PORTHOS

Hercule de Bouillancour!

COQUENARD

And you are garrisoned—?

URSULA

(whispering to him) In the province.

PORTHOS

Ah, Pondichery.

COQUENARD

And you came with permission—?

PORTHOS

No, I came without permission.

COQUENARD

Comment! Now that's my little cousin!

URSULA

Who, as he arrived, brought me back my spaniel—which he found!

COQUENARD

Is that lucky!

(to himself) I'll save on my starling.

(suddenly) Ah, the Devil! And his part of the inheritance.

URSULA

(low to Porthos) Fie, Sir! How ugly to tell such gross lies to my husband!

PORTHOS

Me?

(aside) This little woman has a magnificent disposition!

COQUENARD

My God! My God! And here I was thinking you were dead.

PORTHOS

You are very good—not yet.

COQUENARD

And you're enjoying good health?

PORTHOS

Not very—I'm never ill—but I suffer from a great indisposition.

COQUENARD

(joyous) Ah! Bah!

PORTHOS

Whose symptoms manifest themselves three or four times a day—though a devilish appetite.

COQUENARD

(aside) Come on, got to prepare mourning for him—

PORTHOS

And wait—a crisis is coming on—you don't have any soup?

COQUENARD

None at all.

PORTHOS

I accept your invitation.

COQUENARD

But—

PORTHOS

Absolutely no ceremony—only for me five or six plates or more.

COQUENARD

(stupefied) Do they feed them all like that at Pondichery—?

PORTHOS

As for my apartment.

URSULA

(low) Sir—

COQUENARD

(excitedly) I have only two bedrooms—mine and that of my wife.

PORTHOS

You must fill yours—I will accommodate myself with that of my cousin.

COQUENARD

Huh?

PORTHOS

(threatening) God's blood—would you be refusing hospitality to a member of your family?

COQUENARD

No, Bouillancour, no.

(to himself) He has a rapier of enormous length.

(looking at Porthos' sword)

URSULA

I am going to give orders for the meal.

PORTHOS

(aside with satisfaction) Ah!

COQUENARD

(very excitedly) That's my business—

(aside) I don't want her to take him at his word—six plates or more.

(aloud) Ursula will keep you company, Bouillancour.

PORTHOS

(aside) Brave man!

URSULA

Not at all! Not at all! First I have to go embrace my spaniel—

(aside) And put on my prettiest dress for dinner.

PORTHOS

(watching her) What eyes!

COQUENARD

(watching Porthos) What health! If he were to catch an indigestion.

(with feeling) But that would cost me too much to give him one.

TOGETHER

(singing) Ah, with all my heart I curse the poor relation—for there he is—installed in my house with no ado at all.

PORTHOS

(aside) O happiness I'm becoming the friend of an old solicitor and here I am with no more ado installed in his house.

URSULA

(aside) Ah—now I feel a terror born in my heart for here he is with no ado whatever installed in my house.

PORTHOS

(aside) This relationship I conceive won't go on for long but all the same I'll cling to my cousin.

(pointing to Coquenard) So long as he's my cousin (they take up the refrain together.)

(Ursula leaves by the right, Coquenard by the left.)

PORTHOS

(alone) By Jupiter! I am in the citadel—bad luck to the garrison! The only way I'll leave your home, solicitor, my enemy—will be equipped head to foot for the siege of La Rochelle—but hurry up—the company of Musketeers—the company of Musketeers, of which I have the honor to be a part—along with Athos and Aramis, my two brothers in arms, my inseparable companions—leaves this very night. So solicitor, take your measures—or rather mine—

(sitting down) "Are you like us?" said Aramis to me this morning. "By God, yes." "Then do as we do," replied Athos. "You know that a Musketeer of the King would be dishonored, shamed—if he brought, especially if paid, for his equipment—if he doesn't owe it to the good graces of a beauty—Duchess, Marquise, president or bourgeois—as in the old days knights held in their hands the scarf of some noble Chatelaine—it's an immemorial tradition in the company of Musketeers and God be praised! We are going to the homes the ladies of our thoughts—Duchesses—if we meet them, we will leave their places through the great gate completely outfitted—and if we meet the Dukes and gentlemen their lackeys—we will leave without an outfit through the window."

(rising) In one way or another they are sure of leaving. And as for me, for my past—I am transported to the home of my Bavarian princess.

(looking around to see no one can hear) Who is no other than the little bourgeois of this lodging whose dog I stole—so as to get to know her.

(forcefully) Oh solicitress, my darling, I shall not leave here without being elegantly outfitted—and by the door—seeing I haven't been raised to leave through the window—and it would cost me to change my habits—let's begin the attack, let's write to this lawyer's wife.

(sits down at the desk and mechanically takes paper and pen) What do I see? My signature! I am not mistaken. It's the IOU I gave to the wife of the furrier in the Rue Ours! The beautiful Philomela Jupin! God's blood—her claim here—with a solicitor—she's avenging herself—she wants to lodge me in the Petit Chalet.

(shouting) I demand time—this paper might get lost—I'll keep it carefully—

(putting it quickly in his pocket) Oh, my little solicitress!

URSULA

(entering from the right) He's still here!

PORTHOS

What do I see! What, my cousin dressed up for me. I'm one of the family.

URSULA

Of the family.

PORTHOS

Nature had sufficed you—since—watch me carefully—nature

does things very well.

(singing) Our Queen is a charming model of graces and divine attractions. Surely there's no prettier hand, sweeter eyes, or finer features—still—despite this array with which she enchants our lords—what she reveals, I wager, is not worth what you are hiding.

(aside) What's with me today—I am full of madrigals.

URSULA

Excuse me—you are not my cousin, sir! You've deceived my husband. I was completely speechless. I let you do it—but it's over—get out—

PORTHOS

Me—get out! You are putting your family out the door?

URSULA

Again?

PORTHOS

What makes you think I am not Hercule, and that the blood of the Bouillancour, doesn't boil in my veins?

URSULA

Come on! My cousin Hercules is small, ugly, red, stupid and he stutters.

PORTHOS

That's too much for one cousin—and you don't find any resemblance?

URSULA

(with enthusiasm) Oh, not at all—you, you are so—

(stops herself) Get out!

PORTHOS

Ah! Excuse me, your husband invited me to supper—and that would cause him pain—

(aside) And me, too.

URSULA

You returned Mimi to me, sir—every time I look at him I will think of you—get out!

PORTHOS

(aside) This cannot end like this—I lack something.

(they look each other over from head to toe)

URSULA

(sighing) Goodbye.

PORTHOS

You want that? Decidedly?

(taking his hat) Goodbye, inhuman beauty. I will kill myself without supper, that's all.

URSULA

Huh? You say—?

PORTHOS

I was saying, my pretty, that I left my home, to blow my brains out—and that it had gone out of my head.

URSULA

Kill yourself! And why?

PORTHOS

(aside) Here I am in sight of my outfit.

(aloud) I am a Musketeer of His Majesty—my company is leaving tomorrow for La Rochelle—and I cannot follow it. Then as an honest pretext to avoid the call up failed me—I found one that I thought sufficient.

URSULA

Why don't you go to La Rochelle instead?

PORTHOS

Impossible, dear beauty, impossible! For a musketeer—it doesn't suffice to have courage, devotion, all the chivalrous virtues—that I've got—you must in addition have—a complete outfit—and that I don't have.

URSULA

Really?

PORTHOS

I've dissipated my pay in several good works—I've given so much to the poor that I find myself in no condition to give to myself.

URSULA

Don't you have friends?

PORTHOS

Oh—I know many ladies more or less well endowed. I could address myself to them—to the little Hungarian Countess of the Place Royale—who wishes me well—but one doesn't accept such services except from the woman that one loves.

URSULA

And you don't love her?

PORTHOS

The proof is that I was en route to heaven when Mimi threw himself between my legs—that animal was unaware of my plans. I wanted to end with a good deed. Heaven has rewarded me—goodbye!

URSULA

You are going?

PORTHOS

To cut the thread of my life—goodbye!

URSULA

(excitedly) And if you had an outfit?

PORTHOS

I wouldn't cut anything at all—but with this suit one can only go to the next world—goodbye.

URSULA

(holding him) Wait—you will go to La Rochelle.

PORTHOS

What do I hear—! Your husband allows you?

URSULA

I have money—lots of money that Mr. Coquenard gave me, on the condition of not spending it without his permission—I will ask him for it later—as if for—

PORTHOS

As if for the kisses to come.

(aside) She's a treasure—of innocence—this little solicitress!

URSULA

Will you accept?

PORTHOS

God's blood—yes, I accept—with both hands.

(aside) I've got my outfit—long live the bourgeois ladies!

URSULA

(after having reflected) You accept—then you love me?

PORTHOS

(aside) Huh? She's right.

(aloud) Yes—with love—the most lively love.

(aside) I really owe her that.

URSULA

With love? Not like my husband, right?

PORTHOS

Ah what a difference—there's nothing in common—since I've seen you—I've never looked at anyone else.

URSULA

(aside) He's like me.

PORTHOS

I've dreamt of you every night.

URSULA

(aside) Like me.

PORTHOS

With you.

URSULA

(aside) With him!

PORTHOS

From that day, my Hungarian Countess seemed ugly to me.

URSULA

(aside) Like my husband does to me!

(aloud) But I love you also?

PORTHOS

That wouldn't astonish me at all.

URSULA

I don't see any harm in it—for when I married they told me—don't love anyone, like your husband—and as I don't love you in the same manner at all—

PORTHOS

That's perfectly reasoned.

URSULA

What joy! Mimi can get lost now—it's all the same to me.

PORTHOS

(aside) I've supplanted the spaniel—that's very flattering—

URSULA

You will have a magnificent outfit—I intend that you will do honor to the king—but now I think of it—it is necessary that you leave?

PORTHOS

Oh—but I will return—constant and faithful—like Mimi—if I am not killed, of course.

URSULA

(terrified) Killed! Then they're fighting at La Rochelle—

PORTHOS

Twenty-four hours a day—the rest of my time will be yours.

URSULA

And it's to go fight that you want this outfit?

PORTHOS

Not for anything else.

URSULA

Then you shan't have it!

PORTHOS

Huh?

URSULA

You cannot leave.

PORTHOS

Huh?

URSULA

I don't want you to be killed.

PORTHOS

Perhaps I will only be wounded.

URSULA

Wounded—what horror! You will stay here—you'll learn to be a solicitor—I will have Biquet kicked out and you will replace him.

PORTHOS

Replace Biquet! You are too good.

URSULA

Instead of a uniform, I am going to bring you my husband's new suit.

PORTHOS

But he won't like that.

(aside) Nor will I.

URSULA

You will stay here—I wish it.

DUO

PORTHOS

(singing) No—in accordance with your wishes—I cannot—really cannot remain around here.
    Valiant musketeer that I am, I'd rather die a hundred times in battle than remain around here.
    Near your gorgeous eyes.

URSULA

Stay I say!
Forever around here.
Forever under my watchful eye.
Stay like a brother.
Do you really prefer to die in battle
Than live well around here?
Isn't it better?
If my husband, who never gets to leave town
Should go run an errand.

Near me you will keep his place—that will be so much fun—for him!

PORTHOS

(allowing himself to be led) (speaking) And for me, too.

REFRAIN, TOGETHER

Stay, I say! etc.

PORTHOS

What a happy destiny
Forever around here
Forever under her watchful eyes.

(singing)

Stay like a brother
Is it so glorious
To go to war?
To live well around here—wouldn't be better?

(Ursula leaves by the left.)

PORTHOS

(alone joyfully) Oh! Yes—God's blood—to live around here—under her watchful eye—that would be a thousand times better.

(interrupting himself) Huh? What's this? What is it you are saying there, coward? I'm looking for an outfit and this ingénue of a solicitress is offering me the dress of a petty clerk! Me, Porthos—the friend of Athos, and Aramis to replace Biquet!

(bowing as if she were there) Madame—you love your relatives too much. I indeed have the honor to present you my respects.

(going to leave)

BIQUET

(entering from the back with a covered basket—bumps into Porthos)

PORTHOS

Watch yourself—clown!

BIQUET

(knocked over) Do you intend to leave the way you came?

PORTHOS

Hey, its that poor Biquet—hello, Biquet, you don't have a good hold on things here—my lad—and if I was ambitious—but don't worry, I'm not—goodbye, Biquet.

BIQUET

What—sir—you are leaving? And the supper?

PORTHOS

The supper?

BIQUET

I have it in this basket.

PORTHOS

(aside) Indeed, if I were to sup? I'd really like to sup—let's eat.

(aloud) Biquet! Here, Biquet! Tell me, Biquet—do they eat well, your solicitors?

BIQUET

Yes, sir—when we have company—but the boss never invites anybody.

PORTHOS

What's in there?

BIQUET

Ah, sir! A repast to mortify a Big-shot. First of all, a haunch of mutton that the boss had second hand.

PORTHOS

Secondhand?

BIQUET

Yes, it came from the leftovers of the Alderman—moreover, a quite fresh stockfish, some chick-peas, some hazel nuts and cheese.

PORTHOS

Cheese and chick-peas! God's blood—throw all that in the street for me.

BIQUET

Sir—what do you mean?

PORTHOS

(taking the basket) What do I mean? You're going to see!

(opening the window and throwing the basket) There, like that.

BIQUET

Ah, God almighty! And the haunch of mutton?

PORTHOS

It will be a passible bargain for the stray dogs—here, Biquet, your voracity interests me, and I intend to make you taste a Musketeer's collation—you know Mignot the restauranteur?

BIQUET

(with a sigh) By reputation only.

PORTHOS

(writing on a notebook that he pulls from his pocket) You are going to tell him to bring the meal whose menu is written here—order for a dozen.

BIQUET

But there will only be four.

PORTHOS

Well! When, there's enough for a dozen—there'll be enough for four.

(giving him the note) Here, my lad—this is how musketeers sup

(sigh) When they sup.

BIQUET

But sir—who will pay for all this?

PORTHOS

Don't worry—it won't be you.

(aside) Nor me—

(aloud) Go—run.

BIQUET

Yes, sir—long live the musketeers! I've been in fear of dying of starvation.

PORTHOS

Now you will be sure of dying of indigestion—it's more fun!

(Biquet leaves by the back running.)

PORTHOS

Ah, indeed—it's even worse in this barracks than at La Jupin's! Yuck—How stingy the bourgeois are! What! When Athos and

Aramis bathe in waves of velours and silks—I wade about in cotton and bear shins! A cavalier built—shaped and sculpted like me! After supper, I am going to the Louvre—to Queen's Court—and look out—the First Duchess that passes before my eyes—I'm gong to carry her off!

PHILOMELA

(entering from the back) Mr. Coquenard, if you please.

PORTHOS

(recoiling) La Jupin!

PHILOMELA

Mr. Porthos here!

PORTHOS

(aside) Ah—God's blood—I'm going to give her what for.

PHILOMELA

(scrutinizing him) So I've finally found you.

PORTHOS

Yes, but to ruin me.

PHILOMELA

What are you saying?

PORTHOS

I say that reclaiming my rank and my dignity, I've broken with merchants, law clerks, and boors of both sexes. I say that like Jupiter, I remount to Olympus to bathe in ambrosia.

PHILOMELA

Oh—really! And your Olympia is in the Rue Buse-Miche!

PORTHOS

Stop there—I came because of you, sweet turtledove. I wanted to pay these 200 wretched pistoles into the hands of the solicitor, Coquenard, which you were going to have him pursue me for—a noble and generous proceeding which indeed smells of the Rue Ours!

PHILOMELA

You know—!

PORTHOS

Ah—that's the way furriers act!

PHILOMELA

(embarrassed) I confess it—I gave way to a momentary feeling of spite—but I came to Mr. Coquenard to withdraw the claim—unknown to my husband. Look, let's make peace, Mr. Porthos, give me your arm and escort me back home—I will present you to Mr. Jupin.

PORTHOS

(in a melancholy tone) It's too late Philomela—in despair over your cruelty, I left my home to blow out my brains.

PHILOMELA

Oh, heavens.

PORTHOS

(aside) This is the second time I was going to blow 'em out today.

(aloud) When destiny cast into my arms a Princess.

PHILOMELA

What are you saying?

PORTHOS

I mean the Spaniel of a Princess.

PHILOMELA

Of a Princess!

PORTHOS

Bavarian by birth and widow of a Palatine—I was hesitating still—between her and you, proud Juno—but the noble—Ramoniska made me understand that a gentleman can no longer accept room and board under the roof of a little merchant's wife—that it was compromising to me—degrading to me—she said it!

PHILOMELA

The insolence!

PORTHOS

And that first of all it was necessary to reimburse you for the 200 pistoles that—

PHILOMELA

Pay me! You don't owe me anything.

PORTHOS

(aside) Bravo! I hit the mark.

(aloud) Still this note I found here—

PHILOMELA

(tearing it from his hands and throwing it in the chimney) There—the fire's not up.

PORTHOS

(aside) Eh! Eh! This like enough to a Duchess.

PHILOMELA

Not being a widow and of a Palatine, and lodging in the Rue Ours one can still throw away a few hundred pistoles—first of all I must warn you that Mr. Jupin is a man inflated with vanity—and then he's a man of character—when I tell him do this—do that—nothing in the world will prevent him from doing it.

PORTHOS

Zounds! What a dazzling chap!

PHILOMELA

You were his guest. He won't allow you to be carried off—he will indeed prevent you from returning to your Bavarian's place.

PORTHOS

To betray my princess!

PHILOMELA

I wish it.

(catching herself) Mr. Jupin wishes it.

PORTHOS

Alas my heart is of the same opinion as Mr. Jupin—but gratitude.

PHILOMELA

Gratitude? What do you owe this Princess?

PORTHOS

First of all—many little things—that you refused me—

(hesitating) Then I had the weakness—man is so weak—

PHILOMELA

You had the weakness—

PORTHOS

To accept the offer of an outfit.

PHILOMELA

Of an outfit—ah! I know—your habits are known—your musketeers habits—it's necessary, to flatter your vanity that an outfit be a woman's homage to you—go away—you are vainglorious.

PORTHOS

It's true we are a company of fops.

PHILOMELA

There are duchesses who've spoiled you—as for me, I am only a bourgeois—I don't give a thing.

PORTHOS

(resigned) You've accustomed me to that—

PHILOMELA

And this princess offered you—

PORTHOS

A uniform of red cotton.

PHILOMELA

Nice present, my word! Mr. Jupin will give you one of velour—

PORTHOS

Come on!

(aloud) What's more a baldric with silver brocade.

PHILOMELA

Of silver? Mr. Jupin will do better—you will have gold brocade—

PORTHOS

(aside) Keep going!

(aloud) What's more, a Norman horse.

PHILOMELA

Some starved worn-out nag! Mr. Lupin is knowledgeable in horses—you will have a superb Spanish jennet.

PORTHOS

(aside) Keep it up.

(aloud) What's more—

PHILOMELA

You will have it—but why this outfit?

PORTHOS

(aside) Plague! Let's not tell her that it is to go to La Rochelle.

(aloud) Tomorrow the king will pass in review his Company of Musketeers and—

PHILOMELA

And I intend that you be brilliant like a sun at this review. I will go to see you pass—that will please Mr. Jupin.

(turning toward the little desk and getting ready to write) Wait! Wait!

PORTHOS

(aside) Ah! I have my outfit—

(singing) What a change—
She thinks of me
What grandeur
pride—nobility
In a bourgeois as well as a King
And with a quick word I made her
a Duchess.
As for the husband
—By God, I swear
Here and now
To make something of him—

(Ursula enters from the left carrying a black suit which she places on a chair near a small table.)

URSULA

Cousin, here's your new clothes.

PHILOMELA

(rising) Huh?

URSULA

(without seeing her) And I'm fixing up Biquet's room for you—

PORTHOS

(low) Let's go wife of Jupin—let's go.

(vainly trying to drag Philomela away)

URSULA

(aside) Someone's here.

PHILOMELA

(looking from the uniforms to Ursula and back)

Would this be your handsome uniform and your Bavarian Princess?

PORTHOS

It's a mistake, wife of Jupin—let's go—

URSULA

Who's this woman?

PHILOMELA

This woman's worth more than you, I think—and first off—who are you, honey?

URSULA

Ursula Coquenard.

PORTHOS

(aside) Watch for the grenade!

PHILOMELA

The little solicitress! You sacrificed me to a solicitress?

URSULA

Might you be the Hungarian Countess?

PHILOMELA

Countess of the Rue Ours—as you are Palatine of the Rue Brise-Miche—I am Philomela Jupin—and no one mocks me with impunity.

(to Porthos) Let's leave.

PORTHOS

Yes—let's go.

URSULA

(to Porthos) Stay.

PORTHOS

(aside) This is becoming interesting.

PHILOMELA

By what right, honey—do you pretend to keep the gentleman?

URSULA

The gentleman is my cousin.

PORTHOS

It's true—yes—I am her cousin.

PHILOMELA

But he's mine, also—

(to Ursula) And yet I don't think I'm of your family.

PORTHOS

Why's that? All the Graces are sisters—you must be at least cousins-german.

(aside) I've got it!

PHILOMELA

Shut up, scoundrel—I intend to confound this little—the proof, honey—the proof that he's your cousin—?

URSULA

Why—that my husband received him.

PHILOMELA

That only proves your husband is an imbecile—we knew that already.

URSULA

What tells me he is your relative?

URSULA

Everyone knows my principles—and that no one but a close relative would I let touch the end of my glove—Porthos kiss my hand!

PORTHOS

(aside) Come—La Jupin must not be given the lie.

URSULA

You take him thus? My cousin, embrace me—like this morning.

PORTHOS

(aside) Nor the little Coquenard either—

URSULA

On my face.

PHILOMELA

What a horror!

PORTHOS

A cousin—it's quite innocent—and then you want proof—we'll give you some—

(he embraces her) That's what it is.

PHILOMELA

You're pushing me to the limits—my cousin—kiss me on the cheek.

PORTHOS

(aside) Ah, why this amuses me very much at the moment.

(he kisses and embraces her) Solid as a rock!

URSULA

On both cheeks, my cousin!

PORTHOS

(aside) Fine with me.

(he kisses her) Soft as satin!

PHILOMELA

Watch out! I won't give in, I warn you of that.

URSULA

Me neither! I tell you in advance.

PORTHOS

(aside) Bravo! Here we have the prude and the ingénue launched.

(The women stop, undecided.)

PORTHOS

(singing) Why—what's stopping you? It was going so well—what?
Are you leaving the test unfinished?

URSULA & PHILOMELA

(singing) But—

PORTHOS

(singing) But what? I submitted to it gaily, this charming game pleases me, yes—surely.
Luckily, I keep all the winnings for myself.

URSULA and PHILOMELA

(singing) But our husbands?

PORTHOS

(singing) Damn! There are two to—

COQUENARD

(outside) Ursula!

URSULA

My husband.

PHILOMELA

Good—I'm going to tell him.

JUPIN

(outside) Philomela.

URSULA

Very fine! He's going to know everything.

PORTHOS

(throwing himself between them) Foolhardies! What are you going to do? Just now I was everybody's cousin—would you now have me be no one's cousin—? First of all—I don't take it on myself to convince these gentleman.

PHILOMELA

(after a silence) Madame Coquenard.

URSULA

Mme. Jupin?

PHILOMELA

(offering her hand) I won't speak except after you.

URSULA

(giving it to her) Be quit, I'll shut up.

PORTHOS

(taking both hands) That's it—we'll arrange the affair in the family.

(Coquenard and Jupin enter from the rear, each carrying a pot of cloves.)

JUPIN

The porter was right! Philomela was here with your wife—they have gotten to know each other.

PORTHOS

They adore each other all ready!

COQUENARD

Jupin, I present to you Mr. Hercule de Bouillancour! Cousin of my wife—

PHILOMELA

Oh! If I don't control myself.

PORTHOS

(low) Control yourself, wife Jupin!

JUPIN

(low) The cousin whose death you fancy?

(he bows) Sir—your health is good? Pretty one, I thought of you—a pot of yellow cloves—your favorite flower.

(he puts it by the chimney)

COQUENARD

(to Ursula) I didn't want to be behind in gallantry I adore bear's ear—but Jupin told me that the clove had the best air—so I took the clove—how this yellow plant gets in my way—

(he puts his pot on a round table near the transept)

JUPIN

Philomela—we are dining here—Coquenard invited me.

COQUENARD

(aside) Actually, he invited himself—

Well, my dear Hercule! I've learned that the musketeers are leaving tomorrow for La Rochelle.

THE TWO WOMEN

(aside, with chagrin) Tomorrow!

COQUENARD

Tonight we'll drink the parting toast.

JUPIN

The company will be dressed brand new—you also must have a luxurious outfit.

PORTHOS

(striking him on the shoulder and smiling) Yes, I expect it.

COQUENARD

(calling) Biquet! The dinner—quick—Jupin—we're still going to set the table.

(they arrange it)

URSULA

(to Porthos) I will tell my husband tonight that you are changing your condition—and you will stay here.

PORTHOS

(low) Yes—dear angel—

PHILOMELA

(low) You won't got to La Rochelle—and you won't stay here.

PORTHOS

(low) No, Philomela.

COQUENARD

I don't know where that Biquet is. Ursula, lay the table.

URSULA

(annoyed) With pleasure.

(returning) Madame Jupin really wants to help me.

PHILOMELA

(annoyed) Certainly.

(The Coquenard and the Jupins open the buffet alternatively and take all they need to lay the table and do so.)

PORTHOS

(aside) Goodbye my outfit and La Rochelle! But by Jove love will pay for Glory—first of all it's necessary to make peace with each of them and obtain a rendezvous—but how to speak with one without the other? Suppose I were to write—? Yes—that's it. During the supper I will find a means to—

(runs to the desk and writes)

JUPIN

You are writing, Musketeer?

PORTHOS

Yes, to two of my friends.

(aside) What signal?

(seeing a pot of flowers by the chimney) Ah—those flowers—I've got it.

(he writes excitedly)

BIQUET

(entering from the rear with plates containing several large servings) Boss—here's the dinner.

COQUENARD

(stunned) What's all this.

BIQUET

It's only the first service.

COQUENARD

(jumping at his throat) Why, hangman! Who ordered all this?

PORTHOS

(leaving the desk) Me.

COQUENARD

And who will pay?

PORTHOS

You.

JUPIN

That's fair.

COQUENARD

(aside) Oh—if you don't leave tomorrow!

PORTHOS

Let's go to table! In my capacity as cousin and guest, I take my place in the middle—Madame Jupin at my right, Madame Coquenard at my left.

PHILOMELA

(aside) Beside her—oh! Not at all—

(aloud) That's it.

(pointing to the extreme left) Madame Coquenard over here—

URSULA

(aside) Ah—oh, yeah!

(aloud pointing to the extremity at the right) Madame Jupin here.

PORTHOS

It's indeed all set?

(as they go to take their chairs he places a note under Ursula's plate, and another under Philomela's)

ALL

Yes—yes.

PORTHOS

Come—let's sit.

ALL

(sitting and singing) Lovely day
Hurry to eat—
This moment
Is charming.
We're going to have
Good cheer.
It's the best
Around here.

(tremolo by the orchestra as the chorus takes up the refrain)

JUPIN

(aside) She's really quite pretty, the little Coquenard.

(aloud) I make a proposal—Coquenard suppose we swap? At supper of course—between husbands you swap.

COQUENARD

(with annoyance) It's all the same to me!

PORTHOS

(aside) May the devil take him!

PHILOMELA

(offering her place and taking Ursula's) What then—Madame?

(Porthos rises with the intention of taking the notes back but Coquenard and Jupin each seize him by the arm and make him sit despite himself.)

URSULA

(offering her place and taking that of Philomela) With the greatest of pleasure.

(she unfolds her napkin, finds the letter and hides it rapidly, feigning a cough) Hum! Hum!

PORTHOS

(aside) The little Coquenard covered it with her hand.

PHILOMELA

(unrolls her napkin and the letter falls out. She covers it rapidly with her foot) What do I see?

PORTHOS

(aside) La Jupin's going to explode.

URSULA and PHILOMELA

A letter from him to me.

PORTHOS

(aside) The storm gathers, the wave is going to burst—if I were to go set a place outside—save yourself if you can.

(he furtively slides his chair on its wheels near the door at the back and squirms out)

THE CHORUS

(refrain) Lovely day, etc.

JUPIN

(intending to drink with Porthos) Well—where the devil is the musketeer?

COQUENARD

(calling very loud) Bouillancour! Bouillancour!

URSULA

(aside) This must be a trick—what could he write me?
No way in front of everyone.

PHILOMELA

(aside) It's a trick asking me for a rendezvous—he's gone to wait for me. But what to do for—

(suddenly with inspiration and disguising a smile) Ah, Mr. Jupin—what is wrong with you?

JUPIN

I have the plan of supplanting the musketeer after this magnificent Capon.

PHILOMELA

(pretending to be frightened) Why you are not well! You're red like a lobster. Mr. Jupin you must take some air and return home—

JUPIN

But—

PHILOMELA

Mr. Jupin—I tell you that you frighten me—your eyes are like burning coals.

URSULA

(joyfully aside) If he could be made to go.

(aloud) The fact is Mr. Jupin has a really bad appearance.

JUPIN

(letting his fork fall) Do I decidedly look ill?

PHILOMELA

You are terrifying.

COQUENARD

He ate too much!

JUPIN

I was just beginning—

COQUENARD

(aside, pushing away the capon) You will never finish.

PHILOMELA

Come on, let's go Mr. Jupin.

URSULA

(with a secret joy) Yes, leave, Mr. Jupin.

JUPIN

(very troubled) But—my cane? My hat?

PHILOMELA

Here it is.

URSULA

There it is.

JUPIN

My pot of cloves.

BIQUET

(giving it to him) Is that it?

PHILOMELA

Yes—yes—Biquet, my friend, support Mr. Jupin until he's down.

JUPIN

(very moved) I'm beginning to believe that you are right. I would really like to be home.

TOGETHER

(Coquenard, Philomela and Ursula) What an appearance. How ghastly he is—

JUPIN

It must be a fever preying on me.

ALL THREE

It's a fever. Go quickly to bed.

JUPIN

It's a fever preying on me. I must hurry—

(He leaves by the back with Philomela and Biquet.)

COQUENARD

(stupefied) Ah, indeed, what could make poor Jupin ill? It can't be the capon he was going to eat.

(looking around and noticing the flower pot on the table by the window) Ah—I've got it—it's this abominable yellow clove—wait, wait—

(he places the flower pot on the ledge of the transept which he opens)

URSULA

(who has read the letter—exploding) Philomela! This letter was for Philomela! These protestations of love—this rendezvous for Philomela! Ah! What horror—!

COQUENARD

(returning) Huh? What's wrong?

URSULA

(without paying attention to him) Oh—I won't stand for it.

COQUENARD

What's the matter? Huh?

URSULA

(excitedly) Mr. Coquenard.

COQUENARD

No—we are along—call me Theodore—you know?

URSULA

Mr. Jupin is your friend, right?

COQUENARD

For the last nineteen years.

URSULA

If he were running a great danger you would try to save him, isn't that true?

COQUENARD

If I could without exposing myself, I don't say—

URSULA

You run no risk.

COQUENARD

Why then I will brave all for him!

URSULA

(gives him the letter) Read!

COQUENARD

Oh—heavens! A letter from Bouillancour to Philomela! The rogue to give her a rendezvous! The bandit proposes for the signal—the flower pot in the window!

(exploding) There—what was I saying—! I really knew that yellow clove.

URSULA

It's really a question of—

COQUENARD

Jupin's confidence in that flower will ruin him! But what the devil do you want me to do to save the wretch?

URSULA

(impatiently) Eh, sir—you ought to know that better than I.

(as he rereads the letter, aside) Ah, I've got it! Mr. Porthos will go to La Rochelle.

(she goes out quickly through the door at the left)

COQUENARD

(seeing her leave) Ursula! She's leaving me without an idea—I am empty of 'em.

(rereading) "Beautiful Philomela—put your husband to bed early—"

(rereading) Beautiful Philomela—put your husband to bed early—

(indignant) Ah! At ten o'clock I will come—if I see in your window the flower pot. Ah, the gallows bird! But what to do? If I—yes, let's take my hat and my cane—from here to Jupin's I'll think of something on the way.

(as he leaves he bumps into Jupin who enters from the back) Oh!

JUPIN

Ah!

COQUENARD

It's him! Ah, my God! How breathless you are—you're no longer sick?

JUPIN

When I got back home, my wife gave me the most satisfying news about my health. It seems that at present I'm very well.

(changing tone) But soon after—she made me privy to more sad news—

COQUENARD

Bah!

(they look at each other with compassion—then each hides behind his back a letter in his hand)

JUPIN

I left my home running in search of an idea.

COQUENARD

Heavens! I was going to leave with the same object.

JUPIN

And I found one on my way.

COQUENARD

I was going looking for one in the same place.

(aside) Poor friend.

JUPIN

(aside) Poor devil! Ah!

COQUENARD

(extending his hand) Jupin, my friend! What did you do with your pot of cloves?

JUPIN

(negligently) I put it near my bed—on some adjacent furniture.

COQUENARD

He persists in his blindness.

JUPIN

And you Coquenard, what have you done with your vase of flowers?

COQUENARD

Oh! Me—I cannot smell that plant—I put it outside on my—

JUPIN

(aside) Ah—the unhappy fellow! He's given the signal.

(sighing very deeply) Ah!

COQUENARD

What's wrong with you, Jupin? That's the second time you've signed deeply.

JUPIN

Oh! Nothing, nothing—it's a habit that I have in the evening.

(aside) My duty is to save him—without disturbing his calm.

COQUENARD

(aside) Let's respect his serenity.

JUPIN

(standing boldly before him) Well?

COQUENARD

(doing likewise) Eh! Eh! What!

JUPIN

Do you know that your cousin, Bouillancour is a charming cavalier—

COQUENARD

(aside) He's putting me on the track.

JUPIN

I am sure if this daredevil goes to La Rochelle he will perform prodigies of valor.

COQUENARD

He'll do it—

JUPIN

Unfortunately he's lacking something for that.

COQUENARD

Nothing—

JUPIN

Yes, indeed—he lacks an outfit.

COQUENARD

Really—

JUPIN

He's not outfitted—my wife assures me of it –

COQUENARD

And you think if he had—that paraphernalia he would leave?

JUPIN

Incontinently—

COQUENARD

(aside) I have an idea. I've found an idea without leaving.

JUPIN

Eh! By Jove—you really ought as a relative—to make him that gift—

COQUENARD

(aside) Huh? What's he mean—? Does this concern me?

(aloud) Just as we met—I was going to give you the same advice.

JUPIN

For goodness sake! As if this were my affair!

(rapping him on the chest) What the devil—you are rich.

COQUENARD

Rich, rich—it seems to me that furriers do very well.

JUPIN

Look—give him—wait—nothing but the uniform—

COQUENARD

If you absolutely wish it—it will be only to please you—and in that case—you at least will furnish him with the horse.

(aside) For you're the one who's in peril.

JUPIN

(hesitating) The horse—the—I won't hide from you that the horse inconveniences me at the moment—but I will impose that expense on myself to do a service to a friend.

(insisting)

JUPIN (continued)

Only for that! For in the end—

(looking at him)

COQUENARD

(looking at Jupin) And I, too.

JUPIN

(the same) Listen, then—

COQUENARD

(sweetly insinuating) For in the end my poor friend—you ought to give him everything.

JUPIN

(getting angry) I ought to give him—nothing!

COQUENARD

Ah! You take it like that! Well! Let him stay in Paris.

JUPIN

Where he's implanted.

COQUENARD

Where he's encrusted.

JUPIN

What's that to me?

COQUENARD

That's not my lookout.

JUPIN

Indeed.

COQUENARD

No—it's you.

JUPIN

No—it's you.

JUPIN and COQUENARD

(together) Here! Here!

(they gave each other a letter from their pocket)

JUPIN

God!

COQUENARD

Heaven!

JUPIN

Philomela!

COQUENARD

Ursula!

JUPIN

The same rendezvous.

COQUENARD

The same flower pot.

JUPIN

(running) I'm giving him the horse.

COQUENARD

I'm giving the uniform.

JUPIN

I give all.

COQUENARD

I give the rest—

TOGETHER

(singing) Terrifying musketeer!
He's making war on me.
He must take all.
By Jove—to get run out of Paris.

(they rush to the back, arguing as to who shall leave first—they leave switching hats)

URSULA

(entering from the left and looking) Mr. Coquenard is no longer here—

(with satisfaction) Ah, he's gone to his friend, Jupin's with that abominable letter, and he's saving him from danger—which threatens his wife—what a scare I had—for Madame Philomela—luckily I was here to protect her.

(suddenly) I am going to spend the evening at her place—and if, despite all, he dares to come—I will see him—

(excitedly) Yes, let's take my cape—my veil—

(she heads toward the right where her cape is placed on a chair)

PORTHOS

(in a low voice entering hurriedly from the back—while she gets dressed up and heads toward the window a little surprised) By Jupiter, the flower pot is on the ledge of the transept—each letter went to its address.

URSULA

(turning) Him!

PORTHOS

Her!

URSULA

It's really you.

PORTHOS

I think the answer is yes.

URSULA

Who told you to come?

PORTHOS

Who? The flower pot.

URSULA

I don't understand.

PORTHOS

Well—well—as for me I understand—that suffices for us.

URSULA

It's Mr. Coquenard who placed that flower.

PORTHOS

(laughing) Himself? She had it put there by her husband—indeed, that serves him right.

URSULA

(calling) Biquet! Biquet!

PORTHOS

What are you doing? What's that signify?

URSULA

That signifies that the Rue Brise-Miche is too near the Rue Ours—it signifies that you will leave for La Rochelle.

(pointing to Biquet who enters from the rear carrying a complete uniform) For here is your outfit.

PORTHOS

(joyfully) God's blood—a complete outfit! I only lack a horse.

(Biquet leaves by the left.)

URSULA

It's in the courtyard—look.

PORTHOS

(looking out the window) A magnificent Norman! And I owe it to you—

(aside) I've got my outfit.

PHILOMELA

(rushing in from the back—seeing them in the distance next to each other) I got here in time.

PORTHOS

(with affection) Eh—well, no, Ursula—now that I love, that I am loved—it is impossible for me to leave Paris.

PHILOMELA

You ar mistaken, Mr. Musketeer.

URSULA

Philomela!

PORTHOS

The fur lady.

PHILOMELA

Fine—nothing will prevent you any longer from going to the siege at La Rochelle—for here's your outfit.

(a valet comes forward bearing the outfit of a musketeer, places it on a seat then leaves by the back)

PORTHOS

A second uniform!

URSULA

(aside) She, too!

PHILOMELA

And your horse is in the courtyard.

PORTHOS

(looking through the window) A second Norman—two outfits and two horses.

PHILOMELA

(aside) She, too.

PORTHOS

But I cannot yet leave Paris without—

(Coquenard and Jupin rush in from the back.)

COQUENARD

(solemnly) You can, Bouillancour.

(Jupin pushes in a valet with a box) For here's your outfit—

PORTHOS

A third uniform.

COQUENARD

And your horse in the Court.

PORTHOS

(looking) A third Norman.

(to himself) Come, I would really be wrong if I delay going.

BIQUET

(running in from the back) Mr. Pathos—Mr. Pathos.

PORTHOS

Porthos—animal!

BIQUET

Two big devils just entered the courtyard shouting that they had seen you enter here and that their names are Rathos and Damis.

PORTHOS

Athos and Aramis. Yes, there they are and both without outfits. They left by the window—as for me, God's blood! I will leave by the door—and all three of us will go to the siege of La Rochelle. Eh! Athos! Aramis—here are two uniforms—hold out your arms—

(he tosses two musketeer outfits out the window) And two good Norman horses offering their backs to you—in saddle my warriors.

TWO VOICES

(outside) Long live Porthos.

PORTHOS

(to Philomela) After the siege of La Rochelle, all-beautiful, I will return to Rue Ours—to give you my custom—

JUPIN

(aside) I'll sell my land.

PORTHOS

(to Ursula) And you, Ursula, will you sometimes think of your cousin Bouillancour?

URSULA

Never, sir—but I will pray everyday for him.

PORTHOS

Master Coquenard, enrich yourself, make your fortune—that will please me.

(low) I promise to marry your widow.

COQUENARD

I won't lend myself to that!

FINAL CHORUS

The Handsome Musketeers
Go against our enemies at La Rochelle
Go to make war
Which they used to do—

—with husbands.

(Porthos steps forward to kiss the hands of Ursula and Philomela—but Coquenard and Jupin push their wives back and take their place—bowing low to the ground—before the laughing musketeers and blows kisses to the two women over the heads of their husbands.)

TABLEAU

CURTAIN

ABOUT THE AUTHOR

Frank J. Morlock has written and translated many plays since retiring from the legal profession in 1992. His translations have also appeared on Project Gutenberg, the Alexandre Dumas Père web page, Literature in the Age of Napoléon, Infinite Artistries.com, and Munsey's (formerly Blackmask). In 2006 he received an award from the North American Jules Verne Society for his translations of Verne's plays. He lives and works in México.

www.ingramcontent.com/pod-product-compliance
Lightning Source LLC
LaVergne TN
LVHW041616070426
835507LV00008B/276